MY FAVOURITE LONDON DEVILS

MY FAVOURITE LONDON DEVILS

IAIN SINCLAIR

with illustrations by
Dave McKean

A Gazetteer
of Books,
Lives &
Brief
Encounters

TANGERINE PRESS / LONDON / 2016

Acknowledgements

Respect and thanks are due to the following publishers, where these Devils first appeared: 'Lost Will' (extract from *Liquid City*, Reaktion, 1999); 'Tick Where it Applies: J.G. Ballard & James Ballard' (extract from *Crash*, BFI, 1999); 'Thin Man Walking' (*Deep Ends: The J.G. Ballard Anthology*, The Terminal Press, 2014); 'Taking Jimmy to Departure' (extract from *London Orbital*, Granta, 2002); 'About Millennium People' (Fourth Estate, 2014); 'The Lowlife (1963)' (Harvill Press, 2001); 'Scamp (1950)' (Five Leaves Publications, 2010); 'Wise Women' (extract from *London Overground*, Hamish Hamilton, 2015); 'Cowboy/Deleted File' (Test Centre, 2013); 'The Secret Agent (1907)' ('Theatre of the City', *Guardian*, 14 July 2005); 'A Study in Scarlet (1887)' (Penguin, 2001); 'Click Click Click: *Hangover Square* (1941)' ('Pulped Fictions', *Guardian*, 12 March 2005); 'The Grass Arena (1988)' ('Monster Doss House', *London Review of Books*, 24 November 1988); 'Gaudy Living' (extract from *Liquid City*, Reaktion, 1999); 'London's Underworld (1912)' (Anthem Press, 2006); 'Lonesome Traveller (1960): Kerouac's London Dérive' (*Beat Scene*, October 2010); 'Our Unknown Everywhere' (*Our Unknown Everywhere: Arthur Machen as Presence*, Three Impostors, 2013); 'Mother London (1988)' (*New Statesman*, 24 June 1988); 'King of the City (2000)' (*London Review of Books*, 30 November 2000); 'Wide Boys Never Work (1937)' (London Books, 2008). Thanks are also due to Jeff Johnson for his help in recovering texts from cold storage. Finally, the publisher wishes to express their gratitude to Mr Sinclair for revising and reworking these pieces especially for this book.

ISBN 978-1-910691-17-5 (paperback)
      978-1-910691-16-8 (hardback)

Second Printing

MY FAVOURITE LONDON DEVILS. COPYRIGHT © 2016 IAIN SINCLAIR
ILLUSTRATIONS. COPYRIGHT © 2016 DAVE McKEAN
FIRST PUBLISHED 2016 BY TANGERINE PRESS
18 RIVERSIDE ROAD
GARRATT BUSINESS PARK
LONDON
SW17 0BA
ENGLAND
eatmytangerine.com
PRINTED & BOUND IN ENGLAND BY CLAYS LTD
ALL RIGHTS RESERVED

Printed on acid-free paper

TABLE OF CONTENTS

RETURNING TO BEYOND WHERE WE'D LIKE TO BE

A series of accidents and an encounter in a winter church in the City of London led me to the submerged rectangular cloister of a Capuchin catacomb in Palermo. To that display of challenging witnesses: the hooked dead, vertical monks and lawyers leaking straw, medical men unable to cure themselves and pale young girls stalled on the threshold of their first communion. Shelves of skulls are more dignified in their anonymity, a bone orchestra of bleached drums soliciting the touch of warm fingers. Soliciting *voice*.

Walking among these mute husks, early and alone, with the weight of their silence and the echoes from the cemetery above drifting down, I was defining the distance between what can be said, or known, and what is beyond the reach of an alien narrator. Intruder. Necro-tourist.

Being so far from my familiar ground, I translated this local difficulty into the impulse to pay some sort of tribute to my own devils, the writers who occupied the territory where I had lived and worked for fifty years. They were not all dead, my scribes – and that prognosis was, in any case, meaningless: their words were out there and they floated like the speech bubbles that refused to emerge from the gaping mouths of the Palermo mummies. The books of these writers, as objects, valued relics, influenced and fed my own. In their fierce independence, these individuals were also a linked community, like the regiment of scarecrow figures trapped in the sad clothes of former times, propped tight against one another, waiting to absorb the heat of those who come to visit them.

Thinking about the London 'police-court missionary' and night-walker, Thomas Holmes, who tramped the streets investigating and recording the biographies of a criminal underclass, I decided that 'villains and wanderers are always present, moving at the edge of things, the limits of visibility.' Which is just where my devils belong. Sometimes bumping against one another, enjoying a meal or a drink, before retreating to the private place where their essential words are found. Most of the London writers were originally, and remain to the end, London readers. Absorbing and adapting.

Laying out my own catacomb of memories, gossip and retrievals from archive, I am conscious of those who have not been pressganged, this time, into the wax museum. The poets: Bill Griffiths, Allen Fisher, Tom Raworth, Lee Harwood (and many more). William Burroughs in those strange years of exile. William Blake, Thomas De Quincey and Daniel Defoe. John Clare in his estranged visits, his Epping Forest entrapment. Milton. Keats. Coleridge. Gerald Kersh. Edgar Allan Poe in childhood. Jack London touring the abyss. Rimbaud. Emanuel Swedenborg. Dylan Thomas. Mary Butts. Doctor John Dee. Robin Cook (Derek Raymond) on the last train with Julian Maclaren-Ross. Samuel Beckett fugue-walking Caledonian Road. James Joyce itching to get away. Alan Moore constructing a dream-trench between Northampton and Lambeth. Francis Stuart making the worst of it in Canning Town. Joseph Conrad in the German Hospital, Graham Road, recovering from the fevers of the Congo. Chris Petit and Patrick Keiller disputing the 'Robinson' mask with Muriel Spark. L-F. Céline's deranged trajectories in *Guignol's Band* and *London Bridge*. T.S. Eliot. David Jones. David Gascoyne. Ford Madox Ford.

They are whispering in my ear, broken quotations lapping and overlapping, while they retain the right to remain at the limits of visibility. *My Favourite London Devils* is about omission, a wake with restricted entry. A teaser for some monumental future gathering as stretched and endless as the city itself. The present volume is therefore a collision of fugitive chapbooks, scavenged extracts making up a preliminary gazetteer. My illegitimate voicings of some of those who have influenced what I have tried to accomplish in wandering this city with notebook and camera. I am proud to have walked in the daze of their witness.

— Iain Sinclair

'William, Bishop of London, hammered on the great door with the stave of his jewelled crozier, and called, in Latin, for all the devils to come out.'

— Julian Rathbone, *The Last English King*

MY FAVOURITE LONDON DEVILS

Peter Ackroyd

THE LOST WILL

I came across Peter Ackroyd for the first time at the old Poetry Society in Earl's Court Square. A brown room so faded, smoke-filtered and beer-puddled that you sensed the imminent arrival of Patrick Hamilton in a melancholy fugue and the sharp disapproval of the ghost of Muriel Spark. This was before Peter started on the novels, on the London project. He was performing poetry influenced by his New York friends, his Cambridge peers.

Now, fifteen years later, he'd been persuaded, rather against his better judgement, to meet a West London neighbour and colleague, Michael Moorcock, at another upstairs poetry event. We were at that time, all three, and at the suggestion of Moorcock, meeting regularly. I was the newcomer to the writing trade, still tainted by my life as a used-book dealer. We talked about the reforgotten. We talked about our city.

This was in Notting Hill, an independent gallery that soon vanished. Moorcock was slumped in the back row, chin resting on the handle of a dandified walking stick. His presence here was an endurable penance, on the promise of a night out with Ackroyd. Between them, for a decade or so, they'd kept the London novel afloat. Ackroyd was frighteningly prolific, but Moorcock started earlier, pretty much in short trousers, editing Kit Carson comics and Tarzan adventures.

His bibliography ran to several hundred entries, many of them comprising niftily recycled works with nothing changed but the title. Mike typed books in three days and exploited all the Grub Street tricks with artfully contrived white spaces and inspirational rushes pouring forth in chemically-boosted twelve-hour séances at the melting typewriter. In his pomp, he tapped directly into the genius of Europe: rhythms, submerged quotations, shifting landscapes and borders. 'Don't worry, Mr Cornelius, you're fixed up destinywise. Drift, drift...' The voice of the narrator, Pyat or Mrs Cornelius (a London spirit as wise and generous, and awkward, as the old ladies of Angela Carter), was the manifestation of place, wheezy with recycled smoke and gloriously untrustworthy.

Ackroyd breezed into the gallery like a visitor from another genre, a self-created emanation, outside time, something lifted from Alan Moore's *The League of Extraordinary Gentlemen*. He was just in time to catch Jeff Nuttall booming towards climax. A vortex of gravy-stained ripeness, sticky body liquors, orgasmic chokes of breath. 'Oh god,' Ackroyd moaned, head in hands. *Mal de mer*. 'One more "fuck" and I'm out of here.'

Launched, mid-monologue, jabbing with his stick, Moorcock led the way into the street, as Peter scampered, with short fast strides to put the nightmare of the poetry reading behind him. They scuttled around the corner to perch in the nearest Italian restaurant. It was elbows-in-ribs cramped, loud, hot as a steam-room. Moorcock suffered from smoke. His red eyes watered. Ackroyd suffered from not smoking. He pulled out a legal document. His latest will. His long-term partner had recently died. He wanted us, since we weren't beneficiaries – we wouldn't be inheriting a paperback from the great library – to witness the document.

Somewhere, after the third or fourth bottle, a slowish night for Peter, the papers slid under chairs. They floated across the restaurant. Waiters were invited to dive under tables, between legs. Nobody in the place knew who these two men were, our finest urban magicians.

Writers who kept the fate of the city in balance. The rescued document was smeared, now, with spaghetti sauce, bootprints, greasy fingermarks.

The rest of the evening, as I recall it, was an eccentric progress. Ackroyd was bounced down a set of wooden stairs after trying to keep the buzz on by infiltrating a private party of braying social vampires. Moorcock was still riffing, every building a prompt: names faces lovers friends. His memories spilled back through Edwardian and Victorian eras: George Moore and Alan Moore, Edgar Rice and William Burroughs, Jack Trevor Story and every other story from Gerald Kersh to Gerald Du Maurier. He knew everybody. Jimmy Ballard. Mervyn Peake. Angus Wilson.

I slid, bonelessly, from an unforgivingly hard-edged German chair in Peter's immaculate flat, outstared by the albino death mask of William Blake. *It was talking to me.* And the graved voice of centuries pitched antiphonally against the chuckles, the looped anecdotes of Moorcock and the nasal grunts of Ackroyd, who was dictating television reviews in his sleep. 'Eastward toward the Starry Wheels. But Westward, a black horror.' And eastward I stumbled, under quilted stars, along the river, towards distant recollections of a house in Hackney.

J.G. Ballard

TICK WHERE IT APPLIES:
J.G. BALLARD & JAMES BALLARD

Kafka reshot in the style of Psycho.
— J.G. Ballard, *Cocaine Nights*

Ballard doesn't like interviews, so he says. He gives more of them these days. He's obliged to, as part of the promotional machinery for the films; it goes with the territory. Busking his way through the *Guardian* gig at the NFT he looks comfortable with fame: lightweight suit, handkerchief flopping out of breast-pocket. 'The ex-RAF look,' Chris Petit calls it. Nic Roeg and Jim Ballard, clubmen who don't belong. Years spent overseas. A reckless taste in shirts put behind them. Sharp intelligence masked by good manners, the drawl of the officer's mess; golden-hour whiskies at a bamboo table, stirred by an overhead fan.

'The ideal interview,' Ballard said, 'is one where I remain silent and you just ask a stream of hundreds of questions.' He prefers it if the interviewer hasn't read the books he's discussing. He dislikes the cult of first editions.

'Answers to a Questionnaire' (issued in the collection *War Fever*) is *echt*-Ballard, the perfect interview: all questions deleted, pick any answers you want and construct your own cut-up scenario. *(3) c/o Terminal 3, London Airport, Heathrow. (19) My greatest ambition is to turn into a TV programme. (25) Already I was convinced I was in the presence of a messianic figure who would help me to penetrate the Nat West deposit account computer codes. (63) He announced that Princess Diana was immortal. (88) Assassination.*

Having read (or reread) most of Ballard's books, I wrote to the man and asked if he'd be prepared to talk to me. (Realising, all too clearly, that my pedagogic research would have already disqualified me for the task ahead). He replied at once, setting up at meeting at his friend Claire Walsh's flat in Goldhawk Road, W12. (I was lucky. Claire knew the City and the East End and was knowledgeable about London fiction. She'd picked up on some strange details in my novels that I'd forgotten and nobody else had ever noticed).

Now my real problems began: was it legitimate to try to unweave biographical fact from the overworked palimpsest of myth and fiction? It was impertinent to draw parallels between *Crash* (novel or film) and Ballard's life. Michael Moorcock, over a long afternoon at the Royal Over-Seas League, had dredged up a mesmerising account of his friendship and alliance with Ballard, their meetings with Burroughs and Borges, sessions in the Swan in Knightsbridge, parties, brawls, visions, arguments; the trip to a wreckers' yard to recover the vehicle in which Ballard had his shunt. Ballard had said, repeatedly, that *Crash* was his most autobiographical book.

So Goldhawk Road, as I explored it, became a septic drain running beneath the projective formalism of David Cronenberg's film. Canada, specifically Toronto, was the place where Ballard's dream went to die. The events that had inspired the original text, the images, the territory, had been replayed in this neo-Sadean version. Parallel times.

I was introduced to Claire who Ballard acknowledged as the inspiration for the fictional Catherine Ballard. And I was sitting opposite the writer J.G. Ballard, who was hugging his mug of coffee, in a friendly, cluttered space (shelves of books), and telling me why he called his fictional other 'James Ballard.' Perhaps the translation to Toronto was necessary, to free the film from the mess of biography, allowing Ballard's primary metaphors to reform in their essential chemical combinations.

London was too full of particulars. The airport prostitute who was also 'a part-time cinema usherette for ever worrying about her small son's defective hearing-aid.' Or the 'courting couples in shop doorways' that Ballard recalled from his early days, driving down Goldhawk Road, visiting this flat in the sixties. He struck me, and I salute him for it, as a man who doesn't like change. The same house, the same work routine; year after year, book after book, heroic solitude, avoidance of literary politics, reputation mongering. The hermit of Shepperton. Last of the Romantics. He toys, now that he can go anywhere he wants, with the notion of moving to Spain, shifting into that brighter part of his fiction: Dali rockscapes, semi-retired Canning Town hoods, Moroccan drugs, amateur pornography and multichannel TV. Sunlight through the slats of afternoon apartments. But he settles for Sundays in Shepherd's Bush.

I scuffle through the streets in my usual fashion, reading the signs and shopfronts, the shifty collages of *laissez-faire* capitalism: a staging post on the road out. Somewhere unnoticed, an overspill of the Bush; TV voice-over freelancers and market traders, sub-academics and city planners spilling to the edge of the map. Flats for mistresses in thirties blocks with curved balconies and marine pretensions. Businesses forced out of the centre and making the best of it before the next visitation from the VAT man. (This is where, in one of those shoebox studios, Mike Reeves shot *The Sorcerers*). The last days before the devastation of the Westfield shopping-mall space platform. And the grand boot-sale clearance of the BBC's post-Savile legacy at White City. Ballard's *Concrete Island* Westway, up on its stilts, was the vestigial flightpath of a city that never happened.

I log a few snapshots: because now everything on the street looks like the answer to one of Ballard's questionnaires. Melville Court, with its hierarchy of white balconies, waiting for binocular man to check out the traffic flow: the cough of diesel, not the mercury drift of the Toronto expressway. A car showroom with the notice: SERIOUS ENQUIRIES ONLY. A silver Porsche and Edward Hopper reproductions on the wall. Flat-roofed, sub-Bauhaus experiments with *trompe l'œil* windows. A modest flat above a Bangladeshi mini-mart. The fiction grows out of this undisclosed, over-familiar urban detritus. Ballard's trick: to forge a poetic out of that which contains least poetry; the mundane, the scruffy, the sonar band beneath language. Goldhawk Road is West London's exhaust pipe. Fantasies of flow, escape, nocturnal motorways circumnavigating Heathrow's perimeter, are contradicted at every step by the basilisk reality of Chiswick and Brentford; road works, gridlock, tired concrete.

I started the conversation by asking Ballard to deliver a short autobiography, in terms of the films he had seen.

BALLARD: *I was born in 1930. I started being taken to the movies in Shanghai when I was about six or seven years old. I've got a feeling that the first film I saw was* Snow White. *A pretty shocking film, actually. Frightened me out of my wits. I've never forgotten it. Pure evil vibrating across the cinema.*

Film-going was in its absolute heyday. My mother, during the school holidays, would often say, 'Would you like to go to the cinema?' I'd say, 'Yeah!' I and the White Russian nanny – we had a whole succession of them – would pile into the car and the chauffeur would take us to downtown Shanghai. And we'd sit in one of those vast empty auditoriums and watch some Hollywood movie.

As a small boy I hated sitting alone. The funny thing is that now I love it. We'd go into the circle. I used to nag my nanny – if I spotted a couple fifty yards away – to get us sitting right next to them.

I saw a lot of films, all the films that Hollywood churned out. Then there was a break during the war. I went to school in Cambridge, at the Leys School, a boarding school...

SINCLAIR: *Malcolm Lowry went there.*

BALLARD: *Yes, he did. We came from a similar background, quite mysteriously. Manchester. Cotton brokers. Very odd that. But, anyway, Cambridge... I used to sneak away whenever I could. I saw French and Italian classic films at the Arts Cinema – '46, '47, '48, '49. I left school and went to King's Medical School. This was the heyday of Hollywood noir movies. I remember going to see* T-Men. *Which only cineastes have heard of. Hard-edged, really tough gangster film. I remember watching that and thinking it's much more important to see* T-Men *than to go and listen to Dr Leavis, or even my own anatomy lecturers. I knew that was part of the emerging culture.*

I shared Ballard's enthusiasm for Anthony Mann. And for *T-Men*, which came from the period when Mann worked with the writer John C. Higgins and the great black-and-white cinematographer John Alton. 'Savage economy' is the quality David Thomson highlighted in these B-pictures of the forties. *T-Men* featured an undercover agent forced to deny his wife in order to maintain a false identity. The mission always comes first, even when you have to silently witness a partner's murder. For Ballard a useful example of bent morality, the strange imperatives of a macho code: counterfeit identities, betrayal of domestic and personal ties, in order to defeat those who would undermine the economy by passing dud coins.

SINCLAIR: *Did you read pulp novels at this time?*
BALLARD: *Not really, no. Not until much later. I think I read Chandler as his books were published. I've always loved Hollywood thrillers. My idea of a perfect evening would be watching* Point Blank. *I actually bought the original of* Point Blank, *the book by Richard Stark. The novel is just a pale shade of the film. So I've never really liked reading thrillers, but I love the films.*
SINCLAIR: *Did Alain Resnais, Chris Marker, and the French New Wave directors influence your writing? The jump-cuts, fractured narratives, the relish for the city, the enthusiasm for comic strips, posters, petrol stations?*

BALLARD: *I don't think they did, to be honest. My first short story was published in 1956/57. And the other stories for the magazine* New Worlds *were also written around that time. I think I was exploring my own space. I don't know whether cinema had much influence.*

I remember going with Claire in '68, whenever it came out, to a special showing of Godard's Week-end — *this was before I wrote* Crash — *at the ICA. I remember thinking: 'He's got it wrong. Godard's got it wrong. He sees the car as the symbol of American capitalism, and the car crash as one of the wounds inflicted by capitalism on the docile purchasers of motor cars; people whose lives are completely modified by Wall Street. Whose sex lives are reduced to the kind of banal banter that you get in advertising commercials.' I thought: 'That's the wrong approach. He's missed the point. He doesn't see that the car is, in fact, a powerful force for good in its perverse way. And even the car crash can be conceived of — in imaginative terms — as a powerful link in the nexus of sex, love, eroticism and death, that lies at the base of our own sexual imagination. With its heart wired into the central nervous system of all human beings.' I knew Godard didn't get it — because he saw the car crash in rather old-fashioned Marxist political terms.*

I felt when I started to write Crash *in about 1970 — when I'd finished* The Atrocity Exhibition *(which contains a lot of forward references to what would become* Crash*) — that I was on a totally different tack. The Godard approach was very specialist.*

But then Alphaville *was a brilliant film, a masterpiece. No question about that. The interior space of* Alphaville *is so wonderful. I wish I could say that had influenced me. I hope it did. I love all those chrome hotels and the great Akim Tamiroff, in his overcoat, sitting sadly on his bed. Eddie Constantine, the glamorous super-hunk. I think originally Godard was going to call it* Tarzan vs. IBM. *I loved that film.*

Week-end and *Crash*. These films seem to sit at either end of a trajectory. If Ballard's story — 'the nexus of sex, love, eroticism and death, that lies at the base of our sexual imagination' — was to be told in a form appropriate to its content, then 1968 was the time to get it done.

The self-confident sloganising of Ballard's rhetoric belonged in the mouth of one of Godard's cultural messengers: Jean-Pierre Melville in *Breathless*, Sam Fuller in *Pierrot le fou*, Brice Parain in *Vivre sa vie*. *Crash*, as a film of the late sixties, in the rough-hewn style of Anthony Balch's Burroughs promos, incorporating found footage, crash demonstrations, might have achieved everything that *Week-end* aspired to: an energised dystopian polemic. And the perverse indolence of Godard's pornographic pastiche would have given some depth to the robotic fatalism of Cronenberg's *Crash*. Both films were in the wrong period.

Ballard responded very positively to *Alphaville* and to Chris Marker's *La Jetée* (for which he wrote an enthusiastic notice in *New Worlds*), because he saw these films as parallel versions of his own work. They didn't inspire him with new ideas or new ways of seeing; they were descriptions, so he felt, of territory he had already mapped. 'A fusion of science fiction, psychological fable and photomontage, creates in its unique way a series of bizarre images of the inner landscapes of time.' Describing *La Jetée*, Ballard might have been writing the blurb for *The Atrocity Exhibition*.

A car crash was the pivotal event in another film of the period, another literary adaptation, Joseph Losey's *Accident*. But, although the setting was pre-Morse Oxford, the technique was diluted Resnais (with Delphine Seyrig, escaped from *Marienbad*, to take a cameo part). Where Morse degenerates into a turgid promotion for the heritage industry (country pubs, gothic colleges, crossword snobbery, collectible cars, resurrected actors well-used to corpsing), *Accident* manipulates time to keep the wrecked car, the sound of breaking glass and tyres on the gravel, as the energy centre. This modified Cubist approach, oblique slivers of evidence reassembled, forward flashes, dialogue and effects used as part of a compositional field, gives some edge to a linear narrative.

The sixties crash was either a rehearsal for, or a reflection of, the Kennedy assassination. Ballard's great favourite, *Point Blank*, contains a vividly realised revenge on the automobile (a phobic Godardian response), when Lee Marvin wrecks a car lot showpiece by reversing into the supports of a flyover. You have to revert to the fifties to understand the pathology of Ballard's relationship to the American dream limousine; either back projection drifts (Hitchcock), during which it would be safe, the car wasn't going anywhere, to indulge in any form of sexual geometry, or the classic monochrome of *Kiss Me Deadly*. Headlights sweeping the curves of the coastal highway. The sound of the power of this heavy machine, under control, taking the tight bends. A naked woman in a trenchcoat holding up her arms.

Godard's *Made in USA* is the film where the paranoid poetic of McCarthyite pulp (Mickey Spillane to Richard Stark and Lionel White) tries to accommodate the realpolitik of the car crash as weapon of social control. *Crash* could have been made in 1967 or 1968 in this fragmented style, in the way that Ballard wrote *The Assassination of Kennedy Considered as a Downhill Motor Race*, but by the time the deal was done in the mid-nineties, he wanted a representation that looked as smooth and unflustered as late Buñuel.

SINCLAIR: *You've described the assassination of President Kennedy as an 'energising event.' Would Godard have seen it in those terms?*
BALLARD: *No, I think the political perspective would have prevented him from doing that. The Kennedy assassination of '63 could be regarded as a detonator. We move from a pre-electronic world, in imaginative terms, into an electronic world. TV really arrived here, colour TV in particular, at that time. You saw things live on television in the mid-to-late sixties. You saw the Vietnam War virtually live. Oswald was shot dead live on TV.*

I remember watching TV with my parents in Manchester in something like 1951. There was only one channel. We looked at a screen the size of a lightbulb. The idea that TV plugged into reality seemed absurd. By the mid-sixties, TV was a window into the world. It was an unfolding in real time.

Television and the suburbs. *Crash* really belongs on TV, on tape, surveillance footage. You need to eliminate the authorial presence.

Ballard was so well tuned to this unedited reality: the dead meditation of channel-hopping at the end of the day's work, taking whatever comes without selection, feeding it back into the evolving text. Postmodernist quotation. A refusal to make cultural judgments. Moorcock said that what disturbed him most about Ballard was the notion 'that the Shanghai camp must have been exactly like a leafy suburb. Part of the psychosis which is driving him – and that's great – came out of the same narrow tendencies that Kingsley Amis had. It sounds like Norbury. It's straight Norbury.'

Chris Petit saw Ballard's Shepperton house as a colonial bungalow. He was dug into, and making the best of, an alien world. Elective internal exile. With TV as the news from elsewhere. American soaps and cop shows pitching a dream gulag that he would never need to visit. *Hawaii Five-O* and *The Man from UNCLE*.

'The odd thing about Ballard,' Petit said, 'is that you'd expect, from the writing of the books, that his movie viewing would be avant-garde. And you could imagine him wanting to see a version of *Crash* filmed by Fassbinder. But then you actually discover that his expectation of cinema is one of wanting to be entertained. And what he actually likes is mainstream American cinema, *Charley Varrick* and *The Getaway*.'

SINCLAIR: *Is Crash a novel of the suburbs?*
BALLARD: *There's a huge bias in the English novel towards the city as subject matter and setting for the novel. I take quite the contrary view, needless to say. I regard the city as a semi-extinct form. London is basically a nineteenth-century city. And the habits of mind appropriate to the nineteenth century, which survive into the novels set in the London of the twentieth century, aren't really appropriate to understanding what is really going on in life today.*

I think the suburbs are more interesting than people will let on. In the suburbs you find uncentred lives. The normal civic structures are not there. So that people have more freedom to explore their own imaginations, their own obsessions. And the discretionary spending power to do so.

There's a sort of airport culture – with its transience, its access to anywhere in the world. Social trends of various kinds tend to reveal themselves first in the suburbs. The transformation of British life by television in the sixties took place, most of all, in the suburbs, when VCRs came in. In the suburbs you have nothing to do except watch TV.

An inner-London, or an inner-city, version of Crash *would be impossible. The logistics just aren't there. The traffic moves too slowly. One doesn't have the imaginative freedom.*

Part of Ballard's charm lies in his perversity, his unashamed espousal (or celebration) of everything that right-thinking liberal humanism opposes: junk TV, cars, vertically stacked housing developments, multistorey car parks, airport sliproads, Helmut Newton, rogue scientists, the narcoleptic conformity of the suburbs, whisky, cigarettes, pin-ups, ennui, alienation, sunshine and suicide. I found myself surrendering quite willingly to these well-honed techno-babble riffs delivered in the tones of Frank Muir in his ripest clubman mode. Weird emphases and rolling chuckles. Ballard has taken the germ of suburban consciousness and allowed it to mutate into something subversive and strange.

Kingsley Amis was a big Ballard supporter.

BALLARD: *I was published by Cape for twenty years and I don't think Tom Maschler ever really understood what I was doing. But he paid attention to people he felt were significant opinion makers. People like Kingsley Amis – who was a great fan of my early stuff like* The Drowned World, *my early stories. He hated* The Atrocity Exhibition. *He loathed it.*

I had a very close relationship with him. He was quite a sharp man, very astute. I don't want to speak ill of the dead. In a way he followed the Arnold Bennett trajectory. The boy from the provinces comes to London. Has a huge integrity and then gets seduced into a world of yachts and the south of France, the Greek islands. That happened to Kingsley, a bit.

When I first met him in '62, I'd just written The Drowned World, *my first novel. He was then in Keats Grove in Hampstead. With Elizabeth*

Jane Howard. I remember we ate meals on our knees. When I'd meet him in London, we'd meet in pubs.

And then, in about two or three years, he started to change. We had to go to hotels and have pink gins. Things were changing. The Atrocity Exhibition *was a book he could never get on with. That never worried me. I just went on doing my own thing. There's not much element of conscious choice, you know. One tends to follow one's obsessions, hunches. It's all laid down years in advance.*

Kingsley Amis was born to be driven, not to drive. *The Atrocity Exhibition*, which already contained all the essential ingredients of *Crash*, would have been deeply offensive to him. Foreign. French influenced. Chopped up. Anti-American. Illiterate, basically. No proper structure. He may have arrived in London from the provinces, from Swansea, on the back of the success of *Lucky Jim* (book and film), but his was the authentic voice of the south London hills. Norbury. A lazy drone successfully translated to the Garrick bark, but it was always there. It's impossible to bleed the birthright of the suburbs out. Which is why, for a long time, nobody could imagine *Crash* being set anywhere except the isthmus between the Westway, Heathrow and Shepperton.

Sandy Lieberson, when he considered producing a version of *Crash*, around the time of its original publication, was insistent. 'It would have to be done here, absolutely. With a good Elizabeth Taylor double.' Chris Petit, much later, discussing *his* ideas for *Crash* with Ballard, pressed for it to be shot within the topography of the London suburbs that Ballard had made his own. But Ballard wouldn't wear it. 'He sees *Crash* as much a Tokyo novel or a Toronto novel as a London novel,' Petit reported. 'I disagree.'

My own feeling is that Ballard was very happy to have Cronenberg move the story to Toronto, to have it shot within a few miles of where the Canadian director lived; because that, in effect, took the heat out of it. *Crash* would be further distanced from any distracting autobiographical aspects, from the probing of journalists. The film would then become the product Ballard scrupulously referred to as 'Cronenberg's *Crash*'. An elegant formalist exercise with a great car-wash scene.

BALLARD: *Jeremy Thomas and Cronenberg told me, about six months before they started shooting, that they would shoot in Toronto. I think at other times they, vaguely, thought of shooting it around London. The original setting. But I thought Toronto was just right, the paradigm of North American cities (although it's not recognised like all the others).*

'Oh, my god, a bit of The Rockford Files, The Streets of San Francisco *and* Kojak, *coming up again.'*

Toronto is anonymous, and most of Cronenberg's films have been set there. Part of the eeriness of his early Toronto films is because you don't know where you are.

Toronto is the subtopian nowhere in which *The Naked Lunch* was recreated. It was like going back into fifties, sixties, seventies television. Without the landmarks. Without the spit and bite of Cronenberg's visceral shockers, the psychically damaged apartment blocks that could have come out of Ballard's *High-Rise*; the shopping malls haunted by vampire agents and remote viewers. The night drives through streets so featureless they operated like a sick-neon labyrinth.

Ballard was delighted to see his novel removed from all the markers that tied it to place, to potentially autobiographical specifics. He suggested that the names he gave to his characters, which were always, I felt, poignant signals of his intentions, were pretty much off the cuff. He doesn't reread his own work and most of his characters are variants on a number of set archetypes, so the names don't matter.

SINCLAIR: *The names of the characters in* Crash *seem coded to me. Is that wishful thinking? Catherine Ballard obviously derives from Catherine Austen (sometimes Austin) in* The Atrocity Exhibition. *Names that float playfully between two great female literary traditions of the nineteenth century: the necrophile romanticism of the Brontës and the domesticated irony, the control, of Jane Austen. With a bit of a nudge in the direction of the car. But you say that 'Catherine' might as well have been 'Claire', if Claire Walsh had been happy with that? Seagrave, surely...*

BALLARD: *Seagrave, of course. There was a landspeed record-breaker in the thirties. I think you're probably right. I don't know about the origin of Vaughan. I think I just wanted a name that was different, you know. That didn't have any obvious associations. This created problems for the French because they can't pronounce it. They pronounce it 'Vogan'.*

SINCLAIR: *What about the Travis/Travers/Traven mutations in* The Atrocity Exhibition?

BALLARD: *That was very self-conscious, based on – Jesus what was his name? Yes, of course. B. Traven. He was used as a mysterious figure. So it was a wonderful name to give to a character who was himself disintegrating into multiple identities. Basically a psychiatrist having a mental or schizophrenic breakdown. I just multiplied variants on his name. Tallis and Traven and so on. But, no, I don't know where Vaughan came from.*

SINCLAIR: *He turns up in* The Atrocity Exhibition. *He was there before* Crash.

BALLARD: *Does he? Yes. He was a sort of psycho. I never read my own stuff. It must have come from there. There was a connection between the two.*

SINCLAIR: *Yes, but how did he arrive the first time? If there is a first time, because I'm convinced all your work is one book.*

BALLARD: *Yes, of course it is. That's true of all readers. One doesn't want to irritate. I think I said years ago that fiction was a brand of neurology. I still believe that. There's always spare processing capacity in the brain. We see that when we sleep, dream. I did record dreams at one period. I based one or two, not many, short stories of mine on dreams. I used to dream, when I was younger, very strangely plotted, story-driven dreams. Some of them made what I felt were good strong story ideas.*

It was the genealogy of one name, Vaughan, that haunted me. There was nothing mysterious about the provenance, once Vaughan's christian name was revealed as 'Robert'. Vaughan the 'scientist as hoodlum', as Ballard called him, was another television spectre, grafted on to avant-garde literature by way of *The Man from UNCLE*. (Leo G. Carroll as 'Mr Waverly' linked this cold war pop art directly to Hitchcock's *North by Northwest*). Robert Vaughn. But what's a missing lower case 'a' between friends? A deleted indefinite article. Vaughn was Hollywood's indefinite article: oily, slick, tight-mouthed, sharp-suited, moving on castors like a Nixon fixer. Better adapted to the small screen, where his defects (of character) could be more artfully husbanded. He always looked like a frame from the Zapruder film. Vaughn had a face designed for remakes. He sneered effectively, as if the trash in which he was forced to earn a quick buck was endured only to fund much subtler pleasures, privileged collections. He was a premature *X-Files* spook, a bent insider.

Robert Vaughn or that reliable British TV heavy, Peter Vaughan? Who got to Ballard first? You can see the Shepperton magus plucking the name from subliminally received credits; some piece of dead television that rolled through late enough at night to bypass the conditioned defence mechanisms. Irritants. The sharpness of the 'V' declining into the nasal snuffle of the 'hn'.

'Vaughan's present role in the stadium seemed that of a film director,' Ballard says of his character when he stages the James Dean crash. Vaughan is always seen as the energiser; he directs the action, acts upon notions which remain latent for James Ballard. Kathy Acker insists that the magnetic field of *Crash* is the relationship between Ballard and Vaughan. 'Ballard's novel is a love letter to Vaughan.' Vaughan as the dark twin, the nigredo in the alchemical wedding. 'The whole film, actually, is Cronenberg's fucking of Ballard.' And so it is: in every sense. Because the experiment can only work through fusion. Director pleasurably fucking the text, guiding actors to play out the turbulent relationship between the co-authors of an event that must disguise its subversive agenda behind a fluid theatrical surface; a cinema of formal gestures, prearranged acts, critical journeys across an alien landscape. 'Increasingly I was convinced,' Ballard wrote, 'that Vaughan was a projection of my own fantasies and obsessions and that in some way I had let him down.'

It's disconcerting to find the identity of the principal character slipping, the letters of his name rearranging themselves, as they do in the sequence of short texts that make up *The Atrocity Exhibition*. Travis/Traven/Tallis: the coding seems, at a pre-conscious level, to press so many buttons. First, as Ballard admits, there was B. Traven, the enigmatic German anarchist who turned up in Mexico; and who, according to rumour, John Huston found standing at the end of his bed, when he was shooting *The Treasure of the Sierra Madre*. Then there was Travis Bickle in *Taxi Driver*, every bit as psychotic as Vaughan. Lindsay Anderson and David Sherwin used Mick Travis as the protagonist for their state of the nation satires – and featured Malcolm McDowell who thereby linked the project to *A Clockwork Orange*. Travis turns up as a character in Cormac McCarthy's *Cities of the Plain*. Walter Tevis wrote *The Man Who Fell to Earth*. X. Trapnel was Anthony Powell's version of the self-mythologising Julian Maclaren-Ross.

To understand the coded meaning of *Crash*, *Crash* as a disguised (disguised because so blatantly signalled) autobiography, you have to look first at the names. James Ballard, of course. The ingenuous, upfront use of his own identity: James Spader (looking like James Hewitt) playing James Ballard. Catherine, who might, had the 'real life' inspiration felt comfortable with it, have been called Claire. The multiple, but contradictory, resonances of Vaughan have already been outlined: psycho and mystic. Then there is Helen Remington. Remington: the trusty stand-up portable on which Ballard hammered out his texts. A name that becomes a surreal metaphor for sex as composition. Remington also suggests America: the painter and the rifle. (Moorcock, summoning up night drives through Notting Hill at the period when Ballard was writing *Crash*, remembers an American woman, 'Helen ... something'). Gabrielle, played by Rosanna Arquette, is gifted with the christian name of a soap star of the day who acted with Ballard in a television documentary that involved plenty of driving and standing around in multi-storey car parks in Luton. Karen, Catherine Ballard's secretary, part of the lesbian sub-plot excised by Cronenberg, has no surname in *Crash*. In her earlier manifestation, in *The Atrocity Exhibition*, she was Karen Novotny. The kind of comic strip tag favoured by Godard, something out of *Alphaville* or *Made in USA*. But there is also a more direct source: a trashy docu-novel called *King's Road* (1971), 'exposing the high life and low life of London's turned-on, beautiful people', written by the Czech 'model' and amateur spook, Mariella Novotny, who had a small role in the Profumo scandal. The book features all the usual elements of sex/dope craziness, including lesbian couplings and voyeurism.

The names, apparently selected at random, play back into what Rick Slaughter calls Ballard's 'ongoing continuum that represents present-day life'. These Godardian masks, names that are found and not invented, anchor the characters to their period. They become shorthand notations in an abandoned diary. It was the huge success of *Empire of the Sun* that gave mainstream literary commentators the opportunity to 'understand' and re-evaluate Ballard in autobiographical terms. Yet, paradoxically, *Empire* is more of a fictional construct, less the story of the development of Ballard's imagination than *Crash* or *The Atrocity Exhibition*. *Empire of the Sun*, persuasively written, strong on all the attributes of memory (including false memory), provides a convenient framework for 'explaining' and domesticating Ballard's psychosis. After *Empire of the Sun*, the early transgressive texts, the compacted novels, the collaged images of guns and bare-breasted women, would be gently revised; the story recast, as the author has every right to do, as *The Kindness of Women*. As Ballard said: 'The past was the first casualty of World War II.'

BALLARD: *People think* Empire of the Sun *is straight autobiography and that therefore they can go back, if they're interested, through my early fiction and reinterpret it. 'Oh, now we know, the swimming pools.'*

Of course in a city like Shanghai there are a lot of drained swimming pools. But I hardly noticed them at the time – any more than the abandoned houses and ruined buildings and the rest of it. Empire of the Sun *is my life seen in the mirror of the fiction prompted by that life.*

I was fifty-five when Empire *was published. As they say, there are no psychopaths after the age of forty. I mean nobody becomes psychopathic after the age of forty. It may be that one calms down a bit. It's a wonderful time to write, when you are really young.*

But after Empire of the Sun *and Spielberg, my life hasn't changed. I live in the same house. I think people expected me to start jet-setting around the world. My life didn't change at all. Claire and I have gone on in the same sort of life I've always lived. I think it's a matter of temperament.*
SINCLAIR: *Were you happy with the film of* Empire of the Sun*?*
BALLARD: *Yes, I was very impressed by it. It's a very imaginative film. It packs a powerful punch. I don't think the Hollywood film has ever come to terms with war – because war runs counter to the whole ethos, the optimistic, positive ethos. Every camera angle, every zoom, the language. The grammar of the Hollywood film is diametrically opposed to the rhythm and grammar of the experience of war: most of the time nothing happens, then something happens that makes everything even worse. But, bearing that in mind, I think* Empire of the Sun *was a remarkable piece of work.*

Spielberg did a very useful job, in terms of Ballard's perceived status: he confirmed, in the most public way, the achievement of a book that had been saluted by all sides of the literary establishment; by Graham Greene and Angela Carter, who saw it as 'that great British novel about the last war for which we've had to wait forty-odd years.' (Spielberg, as if in response to Ballard's strictures about Hollywood and war, threw himself, for the first twenty minutes of *Saving Private Ryan*, into an orgy of orchestrated hyper-realism, flying limbs, infernal sound and fractured rhythms).

Unusually for a contemporary British author, Ballard has been accorded two pseudo-biographies, respectable films made by men who wanted to do something more than exploit literary properties. He could enjoy, with characteristic generosity, the account of his fabulous childhood in the dream city of Shanghai and the urban fringe nightmare of *Crash*, the 'interior' poetic of his underground cult years, presented as an elegant exercise in Sadean philosophical tableaux. Exorcised (or celebrated), the franchised depiction of memory freed him to begin work on the less frantic, more 'feminised' books of late middle-age. While Cronenberg, sharing a start in dystopian polemic, low budget shockers that were the urgent equivalent of Ballard's compacted novels, and having paid his dues to the modernist canon, had also placed himself in a position where he could, if he wished, readdress and revise his own.

THIN MAN WALKING

The highlight of the Barbican show that launched *London Orbital* was the appearance of J.G. Ballard: announced but never delivered. The idea was to set up a three-dimensional version of a book that trundled around the acoustic footprints of London's orbital motor-way, the M25. Characters, lightly mythologized in the text, would take to the stage, standing firm, visibly present, in their living breathing meat identities. The sound-sampling art guerrilla, burner of a million pounds, Bill Drummond, was on the card. As was his partner in mischief, tank commander and painter, Jimmy Cauty. Bill, a good naturalist, had walked with us from the flaccid Millennium Dome tent to the motorway. Which he kissed with papal devotion. In his anorak pocket he carried the Unabomber's testimony like he meant it. Like an instructional manual.

And there were many others of note in this cultural music-hall extravaganza: the Hell's Angel and Anglo-Saxon scholar-poet Bill Griffiths played some Mahler on a grand piano. The boys from Wire, including Bruce Gilbert, regrouped in sombre threads to do their computer surgery, keeping their backs to the audience for as long as was possible. Chris Petit finally solved the riddle of the road, after the film we made for Channel 4 was over: keep the cameras rolling. Private surveillance footage, no cuts, round the entire loop of the M25, day into night, played as backdrop on three screens.

But the truth was that the whole gig hung on Ballard, who had become a fugitive absence, a phantom outline in the neurotic swirl of literary promotions at the centre of the city. When his books were published, he might undertake a public conversation, somewhere like the ICA or the South Bank. The fact that he'd been persuaded to talk, on stage, with Chris Petit and myself, was the act that gave a necessary impetus to the Barbican show. Jim even turned out for a pre-event interview for one of the broadsheets, on his own terms, in the Hilton in Shepherd's Bush. Anonymous conference room: standard debriefing. Spook stuff followed by an evidence photograph in the rain. Enough to ensure that the Barbican was sold out; every seat would now be dressed with white paper giving the punters the bad news.

Mid-morning. Day of show. Paul Smith, the promoter, counter-cultural fixer and facilitator, rang me. He had received a fax from Shepperton: Ballard was unwell, he wouldn't be coming. Panic. Horror. Meltdown. Regrouping. Paul got Ballard on the phone and offered a top-of-the-range limo, door to door. An armchair on stage. Ten minutes of gentle chat and away, home. Sorry. Ballard was not for turning. I knew that once his mind was made up, that was it.

I'm not sure who had the idea, myself or my wife (she's claiming the credit); but one of us thought that we could produce a lifesize photographic facsimile, a cutout Ballard, position it on stage, and feature a reading of 'What I Believe.' This hypnotic poem-creed was already an important part of our motorway film.

I believe in the power of the imagination to remake the world, to release the truth within us, to hold back the night, to transcend death, to charm motorways, to ingratiate ourselves with birds, to enlist the confessions of madmen... I believe in my own obsessions, in the beauty of the car...

In a mysterious way, as a thin double, a monochrome fetch, Ballard *was* there, absorbing the voices, the tyres on the wet road, the thumps and twangs of concrete music. The cardboard off-cut frowned. With good reason. The photograph we used was a blow-up from the broadsheet shot taken on a traffic island, outside the Hilton. Jim was not happy. 'One more, one more,' bleated the lensman. Urgent traffic splashed through puddles. With raincoat and hat, Ballard was the classic LA private eye. He had solved the most pressing problem of urban life and found a parking space. And he was going straight back to it.

Enough. The cutout signals annoyance. Talking was permitted, in the right neutral setting, under laboratory conditions. Interviews were fine, but best conducted on the telephone. Ballard had made an art form of long transatlantic chats with fans and fanzines. In the later years, there were more interviews than books. Yet again, Jim anticipated the way the market would move.

Ballard came home with me. He didn't blink. He watched. He lay, eyes open, on a high bunk, spine resting on a mound of books, head pillowed on film cans. When the man from the *Guardian* inspected the house, he mentioned this pasteboard spectre. He said that a cutout William Burroughs watched over my desk. They knew each other, of course, but they were very different men. Becoming a ghost of delayed image on card made the posthumous Ballard feel more like that great alien, *El Hombre Invisible*, the man who introduced *The Atrocity Exhibition* (as *Love & Napalm: Export U.S.A*) into America. 'This magnification of image to the point where it becomes unrecognizable is a key note of *Love & Napalm*,' Burroughs said.

I understood that the cardboard Ballard was a passerine, he wouldn't be lodging for too many years in Hackney. The figure had acquired a life of its own. Burroughs saw photography as an occult act. He spoke about the 'image vine', the way that any image implies the next, drawing the narrative on from, say, St Louis to Mexico City. With the old analogue technology Burroughs favoured, the operative tries to anticipate the future moment. *He hit the button just ahead of the thing he wanted.* The future was a fix, it had already happened. The expression on Ballard's troubled face, stepping off the traffic island, portends whatever is coming down the hill from Holland Park, bad things from the east.

I curated the cutout with photographs from the Barbican performance and exhibited it in a pop-up shop being operated by The Test Centre in Stoke Newington. A new resting place, the right one I'm sure, was found. The phantom Ballard would be tripping to Toronto, the location to which *Crash* had been transferred by David Cronenberg. Homeless at home. Hello Canada.

TAKING JIMMY TO DEPARTURE

It was decided, in the way that our negotiations with the world now come, to carry a lifesize, chopped-off-at-the-waist, photo-on-card J.G. Ballard to the airport. A very slim portrait of writer as savage detective: fedora, raincoat, attitude. A man trapped on a traffic island in Shepherd's Bush in the rain. Don't ask me to explain how an attempt to clear a *little* of my archive by way of a pop-up shop in Stoke Newington, once a nest of landlocked Sea Cadets, carried with it the obligation to transport an icon of a dead writer to the departure lounge at Silvertown. A place, I'm pretty sure, Ballard had never previously visited. But he knew what it would become, a suitable zone for *High-Rise*.

My minder, so he told me, had the ambition – he'd been knocked back five times, but he kept applying – to play the part of a Victorian policeman in the fake Baker Street property where Sherlock Holmes never lived. The boy was supremely qualified: height, weight, silence. Even his brutally polished black shoes made him look like one of those undercover cops sent to infiltrate climate protest cabals and animal rights attics. On the understanding that they can sleep with all the women. He made me think of the thing Herbert Huncke said about Burroughs: 'That guy's *heat*.' Stanley's original clothes had vanished when he was expelled from a Brixton squat, so he stayed in riot-squad black with a wool cap. He carried a dozen identity cards and picked his name according to the season. He said he would tap dance naked in public, but never utter a word of explanation before screening some Balkan classic without subtitles. When he put his arm around the spectral cutout Ballard, it looked as if he had him banged to rights. He was taking him into custody.

In life, the author of *High-Rise* stayed close to the ground, out west, on a weekend stretch of the Thames favoured by Edwardian adulterers. He was driven, once, to take a look at the contentless folly of the Millennium Dome – and he adapted the title for one of his later books. But the whole sorry psychodrama of Docklands, Thames Gateway, spillage and storage, was a plodding footnote to Ballard's dazzling fictional projections. If he had now to be shipped to a collector in Toronto, he was only following in the footprints of the film of *Crash*. The downriver zone, landfill and container stack, is royally fucked. *High-Rise* without the canine barbecues. Stanley set up a pocket-camera surveillance system, spook stuff, and I snapped away.

Climbing aboard the Overground railway, the picture is the story. Ballard in Whitechapel? A boy on the DLR recognised the cutout and wondered why. Walking from Greenwich to the Dome seemed right. Holding the cardboard figure aloft on the ley line running from General Wolfe's statue on the hill to St Anne's in Limehouse, I could feel blood-heat enter the paper. I could feel the beat of a telltale heart. Confirmation of life beyond life: the immortality of the perfectly crafted novel.

We took a generic coffee beside the Dome, outside, at a table where Stanley could manipulate a toothpick-thin ciggie. Then we collected our boarding passes for the Emirates Airline chairlift to the north shore. The pods were empty. The flight attendants were in tight uniforms and full slap. The invitation to a post-Ballardian orgy scenario was over-whelming. The fixed expression of the cutout became an exercise in montage: how the same face, placed against different backdrops, registers infinite discriminations of horror. And rather enjoys it. The future is cancelling itself out in a series of tired fictions Xeroxed from Ballard texts.

Armed police had taken over the area of the City Airport where Derek Raymond once greeted Martin Stone, beret to beret, before they drank the complimentary bar dry of Guinness. We checked the departures board, booked Ballard in, business class, and then I left Stanley to it. London felt emptier for this double absence. I'd flogged my old portable typewriter at the Sea Cadets' building. I hadn't used it in years. But now that it was gone, I'd forgotten how to write in that way. I was taking the dictation of cardboard cutouts. I was composing catalogues not literature. And this too was a sort of homage to Ballard. He made the list into an art form. Post-mortem, he was our surest guide to Millennium City and the Isle of Dogs.

ABOUT *MILLENNIUM PEOPLE* (2003)

The classic Ballard equation, smoothed to essence by repetition, does not surrender the ability to shock. A signature effect transmitted through elegant statements of the obvious. Originality is where we least expect to find it, in plain sight, in folds of the map lifted straight from estate agents' brochures and partial reports on morning radio. Of the great twentieth-century nihilists, Ballard has more to say about William Burroughs, as mentor and shadow twin, than Samuel Beckett. But all three writers, in their different guises, are initiates of the abyss, the black hole at the edge of millennial consciousness. They stared at it and it stared right back. In his 1931 essay on Proust, Beckett explains how it is necessary 'to examine in the first place that double-headed monster of damnation and salvation – Time.' The ability to travel without obvious strain, instantaneously, both ways in time, is a measure of the contemporary master.

When commentators assumed, after the public triumph of *Empire of the Sun* (1984), that the Ballardian code was cracked, that the drained swimming pools, perimeter fences around airfields, barbarities occurring among dreaming villas with immaculate lawns, were now explained, the author smiled. Details in the final autobiography, *Miracles of Life* (2008), revised the picture again. Now his family were with young Jimmy in the Shanghai internment camp. Now there was a sister to be stared at through the eyehole of a large plywood screen placed at the centre of the dining table. 'A miniature hatch cover that I would flick into place when she noticed my staring eye.' Cruelty. Black humour. That infamous sliced eye metaphor, cloud across moon, in *Un Chien Andalou*, the film-poem by Buñuel and Dali, domesticated by the perverse genius of Ballard.

The hieratic rituals of middle-class life in pre-war Shanghai were more Surrey than Surrey. As a boy, Ballard enjoyed the unreal privileges of ex-pat existence in an enclave within an enclave, a trading port with architectural elements of Liverpool and décor by Joseph von Sternberg. The future novelist was gifted with outsider status. He became a recording eye, noticing everything, feeling nothing, when he was driven to the cinema with Vera, his white Russian nanny. 'The honour guard of fifty Chinese hunchbacks outside the film premiere of *The Hunchback of Notre Dame* sticks in my mind.' Progress through the crowded streets was a complex tracking shot of still images fixed in a living present, but accessible for future routines.

Reflex tourism, by way of shopping mall, duty-free airport, is one of the prime targets of Ballard's savage comedy, *Millennium People*. Some voices at the time of original publication were uncomfortable with the Shepperton author's return to London as a set: his prescient satire on gated communities, the terminal uniformity of television, the unblushing mendacity of politicians, the sinister psychopathology of police and Secret State. Ballard, they felt, was not to be trusted as a critic of St John's Wood, the National Film Theatre, Tate Modern, the London Eye. They were quite wrong. As *Millennium People* demonstrates *Ballard is the authentic London eye*. Undeceived. Unblinking. Witness to a city in the process of losing its soul. The distinction between drowsy riparian settlements of the Thames Valley and the incomers at the fictional Chelsea Marina (neither in Chelsea, nor a marina), was meaningless. Ballard imported suburban anxieties into a capital traumatised between the anti-metropolitan stance of Margaret Thatcher and the bogus piety of Tony Blair and New Labour.

A half-crazed biker-vicar, addicted to the afterflush of whippings he has endured, is a significant presence among the incendiarists and doorstep assassins of SW3. Fundamentalism of every stamp, including the fundamental decencies of the old Surrey stockbroker belt (now given over to Russian oligarchs and Premier League footballers), is suspect. Bourgeois marriage is a lie. Property is debt. So firebomb a travel agency. Burn down a video-rental store. Leave a fissile art book on the open shelves of the Tate Modern shop, its true hub. 'A vicious boredom ruled the world, for the first time in human history, interrupted by meaningless acts of violence.'

One aspect of Ballard's years of apparent exile in Shepperton – actually a strategic retreat to cut out inessentials and facilitate a monkish production of texts – was his virtuosity with the telephone. He kept clear of personal computers, leaving all that to his partner, Claire Walsh. He wrote in longhand. But he downloaded his own tool against boredom: the interview, often transatlantic, as an art form. Afternoons in the modest camouflage of Old Charlton Road are passed in dialogue with some remote and unseen interrogator. Ballard riffs, seamlessly, rehearsing future novels; provocative takes on US politics, Vietnam, Iraq, oil, television, Francis Bacon, pornography.

'I sometimes think that in a sense we're entering a New Dark Age. The lights are full on, but there's an *inner darkness*,' he told V. Vale in 2004. 'The flight of reason leaves people with these partly conscious notions that perhaps they can rely on the *irrational*. Psychopathology offers a better guarantor of freedom from cant and bullshit and sales commercials that fill the ether every moment of the day,' he improvises. 'One can almost choose to indulge in a mode of psychopathic behaviour without any sort of moral inhibition at all.'

Ballard the moralist became more radical as he got older, as Michael Moorcock, his *New Worlds* colleague from the sixties, noticed. The novels, smoother on the surface, were now close to genre fiction. This lightly worn disguise – page-turning economy in the spirit of Simenon, with backdrops from the *Cluedo* England of Agatha Christie – was as subversive as the fractured modernism of *The Atrocity Exhibition*. Perhaps more so. Ballard's millennial bestsellers in their metallic silver jackets, looking like techno-thrillers by Len Deighton, lulled casual readers into fugues of complacency. A malign rewiring of liberal attitudes towards ecology, education and political correctness could be achieved without the anaesthetized patient noticing the first fatal cut.

Above all, as he frequently stated, Ballard remained a displaced painter, a fastidious image-maker, an elective surrealist. He was the prose Paul Delvaux. David Markham, the narrator of *Millennium People*, shares a *visual* addiction to the erotic potential of his wife's psychosomatic disability, her use of walking canes as a weapon of power in the relationship, with Buñuel. He must have delighted when the old Spanish film-maker exposed Catherine Deneuve's callipers to our gaze in *Tristana*.

Cinema, infecting Ballard, from those memories of childhood expeditions in Shanghai, through afternoons avoiding his medical studies in Cambridge, becomes the defining aspect of millennial London: a goad for acts of urban terrorism. Like the motorcar, cinema was a twentieth-century phenomenon: its usefulness was over, the heroic period was done. A sentimental attachment to past masters is registered as a badge of bourgeois self-satisfaction. A punishable confession of pernicious *Guardian*-grazing cultural orthodoxy.

'I remembered the quirky young woman I had met at the National Film Theatre, and invited to a late-screening of Antonioni's *Passenger*,' Ballard writes. Seduced by the feral but lizardly sexuality of a film studies lecturer, with posters of Kurosawa samurai and the screaming woman from *Battleship Potemkin* on the walls of her unruly flat, Markham is soon a passenger of another kind, a participant in attacks on video shops. Part of the outer circle of the group responsible for a bomb left in the National Film Theatre.

Readers who had tracked Ballard's work for years, and taken his published interviews at face value, trusted him as a guide to the airport margin, the terrain covered by those lists he delivered like a repeat Ocado order: science parks, retail parks, marinas, golf courses, executive housing, pharmaceutical research facilities, motorway junctions. The internalized terrain of the final Ballard novel, *Kingdom Come* (2006), was the apotheosis of the M25. The Swiftian island of a super-mall is the setting for a mirthless comedy of messianic consumerism.

Millennium People was more troubling because it played its fate game in a city that Ballard had always told us was devoid of interest, a wasteland. A suitable location for apocalyptic fantasy of the sort previously contrived by Richard Jefferies in *After London* (1885). Jefferies imagined his own drowned world, a poisonous swamp occupied by stunted inbreeds. Ballard, at the start of his career, concentrated on what would happen on the far side of ecological catastrophe: London frozen, burnt, returned to the Mesozoic era. He compared his Westway overpass with the ruined temples of Ankor Wat: 'a stone dream that will never awake.'

'I regard the city as a semi-extinct form,' Ballard told me in an interview for a book on David Cronenberg's film of *Crash*. 'London is basically a nineteenth-century city. And the habits of mind appropriate to the nineteenth century, which survive into the novels set in London in the twentieth century, aren't really appropriate to understanding what is going on today.'

Terror and prophecy. The interrogation of the freeze-frame assassination. Cubist scraps of torn newspaper. Silent television monitors in kebab houses. Documentary or drama? 'The Jaguar pulled in beside us, and the nun stepped out... I noticed a bearded figure in a white raincoat outside the Accident and Emergency entrance. He was staring over the heads of the police and ambulance drivers, eyes fixed on the silent sky, as if expecting a long-awaited aircraft to fly over the hospital and break the spell. He carried a woman's handbag.'

Urban horror incubates, unseen, in a claustrophobic labyrinth. Joseph Conrad in *The Secret Agent* (1907). The microclimate of Deptford captured by Paul Theroux in *The Family Arsenal* (1976). And now Ballard's *Millennium People*. Writers, coming to terms with the unquantifiable mystery of London, discover a compulsive inclination towards nihilistic violence. Atrocity as energy. 'If you think blowing up Nelson's column is crazy why did you put the bomb in Euston?' says one of Theroux's characters. Ballard respects Beckett's vision of time as a 'double-headed monster of damnation and salvation', simultaneously addressing past and future. Reports of anarchist incidents, random killings in quiet Berkshire towns, bombs in department stores and railway terminals, shape the trajectory of literary fiction: fictions that, by some inexplicable magic, become mantic, prophesying – *and making inevitable* – coming disasters.

Don DeLillo, a writer who would subsequently, in *Falling Man* (2007), compose a novel around the photograph of a figure plunging through the smoke of one of the burning towers, anticipated the confusion of the September 11 attack, more than twenty years before the event, in *Players* (1977). A group of characters, sharp as off-cuts from *Mad Men*, take their drinks up to the roof. 'It's to give Pammy a look at the World Trade Center whenever she's depressed,' the host says. 'It gets her going again.' And then: 'It's collapsed right in on us. It's ahead of schedule.' And then: 'That plane looks like it's going to hit.'

This kind of hypnagogic foreshadowing of future headlines is one of Ballard's great gifts. His forensic prose has journalists ringing him for quotes every time there is a car crash in an underpass or a detonated airliner seems to confirm a speculative thesis. The framing narrative of *Millennium People* is built from a close reading of recent outrages: the unsolved murder of the television presenter Jill Dando on her Fulham doorstep, the Hungerford killings by Michael Ryan, the massacre of sixteen children and one adult at Dunblane Primary School on 13 March 1996. Ballard's Chelsea Marina cultists, disaffected middle-class professionals, repeat the Dando assassination like a television re-enactment. The rogue paediatrician, Richard Gould, heretical prophet of the group, makes regular pilgrimages to Hungerford.

The names Ballard gives his actors are always significant. The narrator of *Crash*, his most celebrated novel of dislocation and perversity in London's motorway edgeland, is called James Ballard. He asked his girlfriend, Claire Walsh, if she'd like Catherine, the character played by Deborah Kara Unger in the Cronenberg film, to have her name. Claire thought not. But the fiercely independent film lecturer in

Millennium People, Kay Churchill does carries Claire's maiden name.

And what do we make of David Markham, the mediating consciousness of *Millennium People*? Is the first name a gesture towards Cronenberg? And the Markham bit, perhaps, a nod to Ballard's early supporter and Hampstead friend, Kingsley Amis? Under the pseudonym 'Robert Markham', Amis wrote the posthumous James Bond novel, *Colonel Sun*. The sun, presented on the Japanese flag seen on the cover of *Empire of the Sun*, has a symbolic role to play in *Millennium People*. There is a weird epiphany for Richard Gould, after the doorstep shooting of the Dando character in Fulham, when he lifts his arms and salutes the burning orb behind the leaves of the trees in Bishop's Park.

Ballard's millennial London is calibrated in ways we can only begin to understand as the years play out and the politics of development and regeneration speed to a critical point. After the mad clergyman has thrown his revolver into the Thames, he vanishes 'into the infinite space of Greater London, a terrain beyond all maps.' At that intersection of time and place, when books and charts can no longer be relied on, Ballard's lean narratives become uncanny. Five years after the publication of his novel, there was a tragic incident in Chelsea that could have been lifted straight from the pages of *Millennium People*. A barrister, Mark Saunders, living in a quiet residential square, just off King's Road, fired his shotgun indiscriminately at neighbours. The police were called. One of the eyewitnesses, Jane Winkworth, was in the private garden, working on shoe designs. Her clients, newspapers reported, had included Diana, Princess of Wales and now Kate Middleton. A police marksman returned fire and Mr Saunders received a fatal wound. *The incident happened in Markham Square.*

'The sirens sounded for many days,' Ballard wrote, 'a melancholy tocsin that became the aural signature of west London.' Producing his novel, right on the hinge of the new millennium, he demonstrated, yet again, a gift for travelling both ways in time, teaching us how to read the runes and how to confront the best as well as the worst of ourselves.

Alexander Baron

THE LOWLIFE (1963)

We live at a time when the pre-forgotten seek out the reforgotten, the old ones, hoping to verify a mythical past. Alexander Baron, when I visited him (with the film-maker Chris Petit) in the tranquillity of his Golders Green retirement, knew very well that the game had changed: he no longer had the publishers' phone numbers, but he kept on writing. That's what he did. What he had always done, since he returned from the war; a D-Day corporal, a former Communist. 'A firebrand,' he called himself, 'an extremist.' Why on earth would we want to talk to him? His books had drifted out of print. Even copies of his first big success, *From the City, From the Plough* (1948), a novel which ran through countless editions, had to be searched out on market stalls or in Isle of Thanet charity pits. Baron's Golders Green, like the Mexican border town in Jim Thompson's *The Getaway*, was a reservation of the living dead. Memory men, indulging a non-specific pain, traced the trajectory of sentiment as far as they could comfortably take it, to the edge of the abyss: Whitechapel. Heritage swamp. Pier of survivors.

We took Baron back to Cheshire Street, to Hare Marsh, the location for *King Dido* (1969), a fierce fable in which a working man rages against his inevitable fate, the taint in stone; the way that certain areas defy redemption. The elderly author, unpublished since 1979, when his Spanish novel, *Franco Is Dying*, met with the indifference that seems to be the lot of any awkward cuss who refuses to step aside when his number's up, was bemused to find himself transported to an unconvincing but oddly familiar set. With his stocky build, silvered hair, fists bunched in the pockets of a white raincoat, he reminded Petit of the actor Lino Ventura in a underworld flick by Jean-Pierre Melville. Baron was physically strong but out of sync with present dereliction and neglect: the corrugated fence, the piles of smouldering rubbish, the feral dogs. To regress, to dredge up reminiscences of post-war Hackney, the family home, months of wandering the streets like a sleepwalker, was visibly stressful. He faced the cameras, square on, but his eyes moved away, tracking a palpable absence.

Something had gone badly wrong. The novels, when Baron discussed them with one of the new generation who found their way to his house – the novelist John Williams, or the researchers Jeb Nichols and Lorraine Morley (*Other Words*, December 1988) – were written by a doppelgänger, a cocky pretender who shared the old man's name. 'You've stirred up memories there,' he would say. This was a *mensch*, modest, soft-spoken, generous with his time. A man who had outlived his expectations. There were no comebacks on the horizon, but Baron's books, so the youthful pilgrims insisted, lived on in the perpetual present of achieved and transformed experience. Reservoirs of darkness can never be dispersed. The Hare Marsh pub, outside which Dido Peach fights, merged with the Carpenter's Arms, a command post for the Kray twins; the backwater from which they set out on the night that Jack 'The Hat' McVitie was killed. Violence feeds on acoustic echoes, fictional templates.

Baron was a true Londoner, which is to say a second-generation immigrant, a professional stranger; the confrontations of urban life were always a major part of his project. His novels are enactments of placed (rather than displaced) autobiography. Favoured geographical zones represent stages in the evolution of the author's sensibility. *King Dido* is Whitechapel, the bloody theatre of survival; the microclimate from which the disenfranchised newcomer has to escape. Aspirant Hackney tolerates the well-crafted fiction of Baron's maturity. Golders Green is the serene garden, the final reservation from which all the mistakes, loves and dramas can be recalled, re-imagined, appeased.

Hackney was where Baron returned when he was demobbed. To his mother's house. A period of wandering the streets, meditative traverses, gave him the time to notice the minute particulars of a ravished landscape, the scams and hustles, the culture shifts. Years later, in 1963, sifting those postwar memories, he would craft *The Lowlife*, his delirious Hackney novel. 'A writer's job,' Baron told Jeb Nichols, 'is to be the spectator who hopes he can see more of the game and try to make sense of it.'

The wonder of *The Lowlife* is that it does justice to a place of so many contradictions, disguises, deceptions, multiple identities. Hackney, I had thought, was defined by being indefinable. A fistful of mercury. Shape it and it spills. A logging of Kingsland Road, which I attempted in *Lights Out for the Territory* (a book of speculative London essays), was redundant before I reached Dalston Junction. Graffiti, as I copied the entries into a notebook, was overpainted; the heavy drench of jerk chicken giving way to the scented fug of Kurdish football clubs. Balkan refugees punting contraband cigarettes blocked my view of a voodoo boutique that was doomed before I could finish counting the shrunken skulls. An old-time manufacturer of bespoke dressing-gowns (think David Kossoff) lived on as a faded sign, partly obscured by a swivelling surveillance camera on a tall pole. Time is thinner (and faster) now. More text, less meaning. *The Lowlife*, with the lean and disciplined structure of old-time social realist television, captures the moment of transition. The known is still known – market gardens, brickworks, oily-fingered industry – but the new life, brought by the West Indians, Bangladeshis, is recognised early, and celebrated.

Harryboy Boas, a gambler and sometime Hofmann presser, lives in a boarding-house (timid/aggressive landlord skulking like a rat in the basement), on the hinge of Dalston and Stoke Newington; between the frenzy of Ridley Road Market and the hushed Hasidic enclave to the north. Harry has a privileged sense of history: as personal experience. He knows that Hackney isn't, properly speaking, the East End. Nobody stays there. It's a staging post on the journey to respectability. (*EastEnders*, the TV soap, accurately replicates the physical outline of squares and pubs that can be found in the borough, but its fabulous demographics – mouthy geezers with a graveyard pallor, nightclub speculators, blacks and Asians as token frame-fillers – belong much further out. In Essex. Romford, Hornchurch, Upminster).

Harry is detached, an observer. He's damaged; compensating for events in his own past that have left him with a nagging sense of loss. He lives in an amnesiac daze, a willed forgetting: existential burnout in the shadow of the Holocaust. Nothing to be done and he's doing it on a daily basis. He has his analgesic rituals: the heavy lunch, long afternoons reading and dozing on the bed; the prostitute, the good cigar. Gambling is risk, inevitable loss. Necessary punishment. It is his only connection to the life of the city, the mob. The scholarship with which Harryboy chases his fancies, three-legged dogs and hobbled nags, is religious. He is a righteous man studying the Torah of the Tote. Temporary wealth, the wad that spoils the hang of a good suit, must be rapidly dispersed, recycled; converted into second-hand literature. Conspicuous charity, hits of sensual pleasure, return Harryboy to the Zen calm of having nothing, no possessions, no attachments, no unfulfilled ambitions.

The Lowlife moves at pace. The mundane domesticity of Harryboy's boarding-house totters on the brink of a Gothic abyss, the half-remembered horrors of Whitechapel and the river. If he should falter, lose faith, hit a bad run at the track, he could be sucked into the abyss, the Jack London nightmare. He would join the animals, fighting for a crust. In one vivid episode, Harryboy takes an excursion to the lower depths: he's toying with respectability, an investment in a slum property. He wins a house, a terrace of houses, on a cut of the cards; then loses everything to an Indian in a Cable Street dive: 'a smell in the café which was like asthma cigarettes.' Alexander Baron foresees Peter Rachman: the treaty of convenience between prostitution, dope, bricks and mortar. The Hackney gambler is advised by Marcia, a tart he sometimes visits: 'Slums. You buy them for the last five years before clearance and stuff them with niggers... You could clean up, Harry. You don't need much capital, you can buy a house for two hundred.' The spit-on-the-palm economics of the city are revealed. Harryboy's unobtrusive, semi-detached life, weeks lying on a bed working his way through Zola, is tenable because another place, the nightland of illicit pleasures, is a 73 bus ride away.

Many East London Jewish writers have left accounts of these transits, shuttling between home (the ghetto) and the lawless cellar (gambling, booze, miscegenation). Bernard Kops in *The World is a Wedding* (1963) links the claustrophobia of family life in Stepney Green with the liberties of Soho bohemia. Roland Camberton, in his Hackney novel *Rain on the Pavements* (1951), sends his young men (arguing about literature and politics, like Harold Pinter's gang in *The Dwarfs*) to Italian cafés where they smoke, discuss Eliot and write bad poetry. Camberton was one of a number of working-class writers patronised by the publisher John Lehmann. The book jacket for Camberton's novel featured a Neo-Romantic composition by John Minton, an independently wealthy cruiser who taught at the Royal College of Art. Minton's Hackney could be anywhere, a generically dingy streetscape through which L.S. Lowry smudges drag their sodden banners. Lehmann's promising young men were supposed to act as salaried spies, Mass-Observers sent out to document the bizarre habits of the insanitary proletariat.

Alexander Baron was never part of that crowd. He met Ashley Smith, author of the day-in-the-life reportage *A City Stirs* (1939), and he knew people who knew Whitechapel authors of an earlier generation, Simon Blumenfeld and Willy Goldman. But it wasn't his business to satirise or complain. Novels dealing with group dynamics, the community, gave way, at the time of *The Lowlife*, to the psychopathology of one recalcitrant individual: a self-punishing moralist, a gambler. Harryboy Boas chases fate as a way of divorcing himself from tradition, religion, family expectations. He's an elective lowlife. An unachieved elitist. An autodidact. And therefore a non-writing writer, an artist of the city, trained to appreciate subtle shifts in mood and weather. Harry, gazing out of his high window, is eager to welcome the next wave of immigrants, but wary of the first signs of the great American consumer push: retail conformity, the suits and cars and sounds that East End hoods customised in their bid for the violence franchise.

British movies, aping the hardboiled style, imported Hollywood heavies to play Jewish wide boys: Richard Widmark, in Jules Dassin's version of Gerald Kersh's *Night and the City*. But the gambling-fever novel traces its lineage to Dostoevsky. It's a well-tested device: the outsider, the believer in arcane systems, divorces himself from righteous society, begs, cheats, lies, steals, subverts every taboo. Revengers set out on his trail. He runs. He tries to borrow. He confronts the mobsters, the professionals of hurt who are out to damage or destroy him. It's a standard riff, a way of giving tension a structure. Think of Anthony Newley, the sleazy, sweating, chain-smoking clipjoint MC in Ken Hughes's film *The Small World of Sammy Lee* (1962). He races from Soho to the family shop in Whitechapel; to his brother, played by Warren Mitchell. Soliciting straight money that can soon be bent, burnt, blown away. Think of James Caan in Karel Reisz's film *The Gambler* (1975).

Back in the Sixties, it was Reisz's translation of Alan Sillitoe's *Saturday Night and Sunday Morning* that helped to marginalise the London lowlife novel. Suddenly the north was sexy. Nottingham, Rotherham, Liverpool, Blackpool: exotic, unknown and interchangeable. Cobbles, canals, industry. Horny-handed toilers with bicycles. Girls (RADA-trained) who couldn't cope with contraception. Oxford graduates, frequently gay or bisexual – Lindsay Anderson, Tony Richardson, John Schlesinger – dusted down the Lehmann trope. London fiction moved away from the Jewish working class (Baron,

Emanuel Litvinoff, Bernard Kops) to those who could talk up the changes, soft-sell the Swinging City. Photographers, pill poppers, property sharks.

The standard gambling novel or film depends on clocks. Phone calls. The cigarette lit from the dying butt. Frantic moves within an ever-tighter urban labyrinth: Gerald Kersh's *Night and the City* (1939), Robert Westerby's *Wide Boys Never Work* (1937). There's a firm structure and a liquid topography. But that isn't Baron's technique. He is so solidly grounded in place, in workaday Hackney. He runs a double narrative, the madness of the track and the betting shop interwoven with the history of a dysfunctional family (suburban ambitions reduced to the declining no-man's-land of Dalston). The child of this family becomes Harryboy's own 'lost' son. Characteristically, Baron spurns the grand finale, the eye that is to be sacrificed to save the child's sight. 'My great gesture fell as flat as all my other great plans.' The Russian novel of doomed souls is therefore reduced to an East London rag-trade copy. There was talk, according to Baron, who had good showbiz connections, about *The Lowlife* being optioned as a film; a vehicle for Harry H. Corbett, the young Steptoe. Comedic/sentimental script by Simpson and Galton? It never happened.

When I pitched out on a Camden Passage bookstall in the mid-Seventies, a speed-freak friend of Malcolm McLaren, who had grown up in the streets Baron describes so lovingly, told me that I should read this 'amazing' book, *The Lowlife*. He was, as usual, quite right. It was as if a direct descendant of Harryboy Boas, a runner, chaser of rumours, a hand-to-mouth man with a powerful appetite for literature and gossip, was recommending the autobiography he would never get around to writing. I picked up the Collins first edition (I don't remember seeing any other) within a few days. The runner talked so fast, quarrelled, embraced, argued, he must have done his reading on the wing: as he jogged between appointments. His taste was excellent. He puffed Colin MacInnes (*Absolute Beginners*), Michael Moorcock, Gerald Kersh, James Curtis. And he led me, with *The Lowlife*, to one of the best fictions, the truest accounts of the borough in which I had lived for ten years. I'm delighted to borrow, now, the runner's belted herringbone coat, to draw deep on his cigarette and to make his pitch. You can find it, this book, the place, the story. Enjoy.

Roland Camberton

SCAMP (1950)

You can't tell a book by its cover, but it's not a bad place to start. The design of the fiction put out by John Lehmann in the late Forties and early Fifties had the heft to complement an edgily cosmopolitan list: Jean-Paul Sartre, Saul Bellow, Gore Vidal, John Dos Passos, Paul Bowles. You could smell fierce French tobacco lingering on tanned pages and sample exotic locations filtered through fugues of premature sex tourism. The books looked good enough to frame, we took the contents on trust. And being by 1975 a trader in forlorn and forgotten literature, I slid copies of two London novels published by Lehmann under my stall; in the fond belief that the John Minton dustwrappers would give them a market value at some unspecified future date.

The novels were credited to someone called Roland Camberton. I set them aside: until the time was right to make the discovery that the most exotic location of all, the true heart of darkness, was on my doorstep in Hackney; a borough of which Camberton was the unrecognized laureate.

Despite the gentile surname, this man wrote within a recognized Jewish tradition: the unsentimental education, the investigation of a wider city and the breaking away from the clinging embrace of an orthodox family. Rites of passage involved expeditions to the real East

End, before sticky experiments with Soho cafés and clubs. Versions of this story with greater or lesser degrees of cynicism and panache would include Simon Blumenfeld's *Jew Boy* (1935), Alexander Baron's *The Lowlife* (1963), *The World is a Wedding* (1963) by Bernard Kops, Emanuel Litvinoff's *A Journey Through a Small Planet* (1972) and even Harold Pinter's *The Dwarfs* (1990). Naturally, the authors denied any familial connection and dismissed the lesser titles in the series as incompetent, fraudulent and not worth ten minutes of any serious reader's time. Baron, more generous than the rest, was interviewed by Ken Worpole as background for Worpole's first book, *Dockers and Detectives* (1983). The Hackney author moved the discussion straight back to Lehmann. 'The people you speak of were all discoveries of John Lehmann, a part of his attempt to find a proletarian literature. This had its condescending side. There is, from Lehmann and his ilk, a homosexual attitude to the working class.'

Litvinoff confirmed this accusation when I talked to him for a film on submerged London writers in 1992. He recalled, when still in uniform and heavy boots, being invited to Lehmann's elegant flat, where the publisher was waiting, draped in a Nöel Coward dressing-gown, drink in hand. There was a vampiric thirst for fresh blood, hard male prose, the subterranea of the city. Lehmann had other sources of income, shadowy business interests; publishing was a superior hobby, a way of meeting fascinating young men. Much of the zest in English fiction comes from rogue individualists looking for new ways to lose money by leaving orphaned books for future scavengers to discover and promote.

One of Lehmann's tricks was to pair off a modest working-class writer with a posh but troubled artist such as Minton. The zones where the tribes collided, in lethal blind dates, were Soho and Fitzrovia. Moneyed dilettantes, professional scroungers and the thirsty dead: shoulder to shoulder, they fought for space at favoured bars. They worked much harder than nine-to-five civilians to promote their own legends to the moment where some other mug would write the book for them. The point, as Dylan Thomas and Julian Maclaren-Ross soon learnt, where you become an actor in the anecdote of a rival is the point where your words are no longer required. It's time to disappear. To play the final card: suicide by other means. The last train to the suburbs. Stiff nights on the bench in the Russell Square Turkish baths. Trembling hands failing to get cold coffee, unspilled, to scabby lips. Late-bohemianism is a career better recollected than experienced.

Scamp, published by Lehmann in 1950, is Roland Camberton's first novel. It is set in Soho, Bloomsbury and Fitzrovia; in the rented rooms, pubs, all-night cafés where the author could well have come across Minton and certainly did lurch against Maclaren-Ross. Ivan Ginsberg occupies a rat-infested bathroom-kitchen, while trying to scam the funds for a stillborn literary magazine. The cancelled cheque stubs of Camberton's own life are an audition for the real business: the manufacturing of fiction.

'Ginsberg found himself confronted with the type-writer... A story a day, that was his minimum task; two thousand words, preferably with a plot, development, a climax, and a twist. After six months of this routine, he was beginning to feel an intense hatred of the short story, in fact, of all writing. What an abominable occupation it was!'

Camberton's prose is feisty, but there is something fugitive about the Hackney writer: if he has broken away from his roots, he knows they will reach out to choke him. The novel is heady with the delusion of freedom, but it's on parole. Delivered like an over-researched thesis, *Scamp* is quietly triumphant about coming into existence, but crushed by the horrible labour of composition. Nobody wants a new recipe for oblivion.

Maclaren-Ross reviewed *Scamp* with withering condescension: 'Mr Camberton, who appears to be devoid of any narrative gift, makes this an excuse for dragging in disconnectedly and to little apparent purpose a series of thinly disguised local or literary celebrities.' One of whom, although he doesn't mention it, is Maclaren-Ross himself, lightly disguised as the 'former commercial traveller' Angus Sternforth Simms. 'That he found time to write at all puzzled the little crowd of habitués which watched him and heard him every evening, with respectful animosity, at his corner of the bar.'

Other notices were more encouraging. *Scamp* won the Somerset Maugham Award for 1951. Maugham took against the other principal contender, *Lucky Jim*, finding Kingsley Amis boorish and provincial. Camberton was invited around to the Ritz to be inspected by his lizardly benefactor. A friend wondered how they had got along. 'Oh, marvellous,' Camberton reported. 'He asked if I wanted tea or whisky. And I said whisky. Maugham said, "That's right, good show! I'm going to have both." And then we put English fiction to the sword.' Maugham left the judging of his prize to a committee. By the time Amis got his turn, winning the prize in 1955, the author of *Scamp* was drifting out of print and into Grub Street anonymity.

The second book is always hard. Camberton, in choosing to set *Rain on the Pavements* (1951) in Hackney, was composing his own obituary. Blackshirt demagogues, the spectres of Oswald Mosley's legions, stalk Ridley Road Market while the exiled author ransacks his memory for an affectionate and exasperated account of an orthodox community in its pre-war lull. Competing voices shout across a crowded kitchen where loyalty to family battles against hairball claustrophobia. The novel unfolds through a sequence of discrete but connected short stories, which fade away into sudden darkness; an untimely return to Poland, erasure, silence.

I suspect that the character of Uncle Jake is a refracted self-portrait by the author. A midnight cyclist and compulsive autodidact, Jake wobbles between ideologies, short-lived enthusiasms. He taps on his nephew's window, asking to share the narrow put-u-up bed. Like Camberton, Jake decides to join the Royal Air Force. He has to get away from everything that makes him what he is.

Jake's guilty secret is that, without letting friends or family know, he has published a novel. And its title is: *Failure*. There is a schizophrenic moment when David Hirsch, the narrator, opens the book written by Camberton's alter ego: 'With what strange feelings David opened the thin, ill-printed, yellow-wrapped volume. It was as though the past itself had been drawn, temporarily but without noticeable change, from the vaults of the museum.'

Then Camberton vanishes, nothing is heard from him again; he publishes no third book. John Minton's dust-wrapper for *Scamp* takes on the jaundiced colouring of the uncut pages of *Failure*. A balding man, left hand in pocket, right hand gripping a furtive typescript, slouches down the cobbles; past the pub, out of the frame, into the wilderness.

I asked Patrick Wright, who had befriended Emanuel Litvinoff and written about his work, what the acerbic old man felt about Camberton. 'He was totally dismissive,' Patrick said. Those two books, Litvinoff reckoned, had nothing to do with the East London he had known as a young man. They were opportunistic, banal. He preferred to remember Wolf Mankowitz. 'Now there was a man who knew how to make money.' As for Camberton's later career, Litvinoff thought he had spotted him once, going into the offices of the *Reader's Digest*, but he couldn't be sure.

Alexander Baron, put by Ken Worpole to recalling the 'Jewish East End writers' of his acquaintance, finished with the Litvinoff brothers. And then, after a long pause, he mentioned one more. 'Oh yes, I'd almost forgotten him: Roland Camberton. I saw him once at a party. I think, like Pinter and myself, he went to Hackney Downs School. I can't remember whose party it was, except that it was somewhere in St John's Wood. I didn't venture very often into these exotic territories. I had this little uneasy chat with Camberton, a strange man. That's it. That's all I know.'

And there it would have finished, with no more information than you could retrieve from the flap of one of Camberton's novels. Born in Manchester in 1921. Brought up in London. Served in the RAF as a wireless mechanic. Worked as teacher, copywriter, translator, tutor, canvasser, publisher's traveller. A future project, an autobiographical book called *Down Hackney*, is floated. But nobody I have spoken to has ever seen a typescript.

The nagging mystery was one of many I worried at, up to the point when I started work on my own memoir, a documentary-fiction called *Hackney, That Rose-Red Empire*. I projected a connection with the author of the book-within-a-book, *Failure*. Camberton's topography, his questing excursions, haunted me; becoming, in their fashion, a kind of model. 'It was necessary to know every alley, every cul-de-sac, every arch, every passageway; every school, every hospital, every church, every synagogue; every police station, every post office, every labour exchange, every lavatory; every curious shop name, every kids' gang, every hiding place, every muttering old man... In fact everything; and having got to know everything, they had to hold this information firmly, to keep abreast of change, to locate the new position of beggars, newsboys, hawkers, street shows, gypsies, political meetings.'

Amen! Huzzah! My mad creed in a single paragraph.

Having absorbed Hackney, its lost rivers, demolished theatres and built-over market gardens, Camberton's continued existence was unnecessary: he had become the spirit of place. And through place, miles walked, he was to be recovered. Or so I excused my failure as literary snoop, unsponsored private eye. Until, in the most unexpected way, the name of the vanished writer jumped out at me. A slender booklet, *Walking the London Scene (Five Walks in the Footsteps of the Beat Generation)* by Sydney R. Davies, dropped on my doormat. Here was permission for a jug of coffee and a rest from my researches. I followed with interest the story of how a person called Douglas Lyne, described as an 'archivist and Chelsea habitué', met William Burroughs. They drink together. Lyne lends Burroughs a pound. Returning from Tangier, the notorious junkie repays the loan. A line of double brandies is fired back in celebration. When the two men meet again, in a pub called The Surprise, they are joined by a third: Henry Cohen.

Lyne decides that they will go back to his flat and make a recording on a creaking reel-to-reel machine. They are now, all three, quite drunk. The man from the pub, Cohen, the one who will operate the recording machine was himself, years ago, a published writer. That might have been the source of his irritation. His books were classically constructed, widely reviewed and completely forgotten. To hide the shame of his alternative career from his strictly religious family, Cohen took another name: *Roland Camberton.*

This Chelsea night must have been one of the most fantastic conjunctions in literary mythology: a posthumous nightmare for Somerset Maugham. William Burroughs, the hierophant of fractured modernism, interrogated by a champion of the local, the specific. Hackney picaresque.

Naturally, I had to track down the tape. It became a grail, all my interests converging on a single elusive object. The full story of that adventure belongs elsewhere. I made contact with Sydney Davies and he arranged a meeting, south of the river, a long way from Chelsea, at the house where Douglas Lyne now lived. Mr Lyne was a person adrift in memory, calling up anecdotes of military life, intertwined with genealogies of the Welsh Marches and musings on the rogue priest, Father Ignatius, who raised a girl from the dead in Wellclose Square. He was a charming and discursive anecdotalist; the years in pubs and clubs had not been wasted. He wouldn't be deflected, by my Camberton probings, from the unravelling of an invisible thread. There were mugs of slow tea and many chocolate biscuits. Mr Lyne, with his swept-back silver hair, trim moustache, milky eye, was like a benevolent General Pinochet.

Roland Camberton – or Henry Cohen, as he had known him – was one of his closest friends. Lyne moved in the post-war Soho world of documentary films, drinking clubs where he mingled with writers, painters, adventurers on the lookout for new islands. 'Johnny Minton was one of us. He did the covers for Henry's books.'

The first meeting between Lyne and Cohen was in Chelsea at the

Pier Hotel. 'All the local mandarins were lolling about,' Lyne told me. 'Dregs and real dregs. With the great Henry. Who was an extremely distinguished-looking Jewish man. Like a great composer. Huge brow. We drank and we chatted away. We bought – it must have been me – a bottle of wine. And we went back to Henry's room. He said, "I've just won a prize. Somerset Maugham has given me £500." Maugham thought Henry was a good storyteller. And he was right. Henry could do colourful characters. He had great warmth. He loved listening to what you had to say, but he didn't like wasting his time doing practical things.'

And so, inch by inch, a narrative of the lost years was teased out. Cohen learnt to write in the Air Force. 'When I had a spare moment in the office,' he told Lyne, 'I would scribble bits and pieces and read them out at lunchtime and see who laughed at which passage. I was quite surprised, they liked my stuff. But the bits I liked they found high-fallutin' and boring.' Coming across an article by John Lehmann in which he said that he was searching for English authors with the urban swagger of Saul Bellow, Cohen decided to make an approach. He took his RAF gratuity and moved west. 'I was spending all my time in Soho. Living it up as far as I could. Drinking. Courting the girls. I'd come from a stuffy orthodox Jewish background. I found Soho life fascinating and I thought other people would want to hear about it. I wrote *Scamp*. And I remembered John Lehmann.'

After *Scamp*, there was talk of a film. But nothing happened. Cohen produced some journalism for trade magazines. He kept his head resolutely down. 'You couldn't say that's what Henry was doing, freelance journalism,' Lyne reported. 'You couldn't ask. Henry wasn't a man who did things. He just ran out of ideas. I should have learnt more from him. I didn't take him seriously. I think he had an interior purpose. He hated to be known. He was a very secretive person.'

The pseudonym Cohen adopted was resolutely non-Jewish. He cast himself as a matinee idol rescued from some forgotten Hollywood programmer witnessed at the Clarence in Lower Clapton. Ronald

Colman, Madeleine Carroll and Roland Camberton in *The Prisoner of Zenda*: such was the fantasy. The reality of this grubbing, scratching post-war era was membership of a literary underclass described by Maclaren-Ross (in a letter to Lehmann) as being made up of those who 'live like rats among the ruins which they themselves have helped to honeycomb.'

The family didn't give up on the decamped eldest son. Lyne remembers an afternoon in his studio flat. This very Hatton Garden sort of chap came around. He had a set of sacrificial knives which he used for cutting animals' throats. Henry jumped up. "This is my brother." The brother said, "I've come to bring you home to Hackney." Henry told me that the same scene happened every week. His father was ill.'

Lyne got married, changed pub, lost touch with his friend. Years later, in Soho, he bumped into Henry again. 'He was with a very attractive woman. I think he must have been knocking about with her for quite a long time. She was very gentile, very county. Enormously devoted to him in a distant kind of way. She didn't like being associated with Soho or drink.'

Cohen said that things were going rather well. 'She's got lots of money. She wants to get married. She's got a house, with hunting and that kind of thing. I go down there. My family have cut me off, they don't want to see me. I can't go on. I don't really have anything to do.'

Roland Camberton had grown into the situation that befell Uncle Jake in the novel written so many years before. 'He lost touch completely with the family... their relationship was quietly wrapped up, as it were, placed in the cupboard of limbo, and locked away.'

Ducking and diving, Henry Cohen had the painful task of reading other people's novels for MGM: could they be turned into films? He brought Douglas Lyne on-board – and Douglas, in return, set Cohen up with a trial, writing copy for EBIS (Engineering in Britain Information Services). 'What's this fellow done?' said the boss. 'A picaresque Soho novel and a book about Hackney.' 'Good god! I can find twenty people to write picaresque novels about Hackney. I want someone who writes dull-as-ditchwater technical material.'

At the end of Cohen's first month, Adrian Seligman who ran the operation told Lyne they were going to have a big party. 'What are we celebrating?' 'Henry's departure. He's a marvellous writer, but it takes him weeks to polish a paragraph.'

After this set-back, news of Henry came by way of an accountant, Leslie Periton. Periton was a partner in the firm of A.T. Chenhalls, who represented Terence Rattigan, Benjamin Britten and Leslie Howard. Lehmann persuaded them to take on the promising young winner of the Somerset Maugham Award. Periton and Lyne had lunch together, once a year. 'Henry was exactly the type Periton wanted,' Lyne said, 'a man who didn't have any interest in making money. Periton probably got him the job at MGM to keep him afloat. Nobody knows if Henry ever wrote anything else under another name. My view is, at the times I ran into him, he was a declining person. He had problems with his inamorata.'

At one of these epic lunches, somewhere in the mid-Sixties, Periton said to Lyne, 'It's all up.' 'What's happened?' 'Henry's not so good. In fact, he's dead.'

Nobody knew the details, aorta, aneurysm. Showing me his inscribed copy of *Scamp*, without the Minton dustwrapper, Lyne was visibly moved. 'Accumulated memories do work their way to the surface. I have a notion Henry married his lady. They had a child. It could be a whole new chapter in Henry's story.'

From time to time, in a half-hearted way, I tried to interest publishers in bringing Camberton back into print. I was an admirer of the series of London Books Classics being put out by John King and his partners. In considering *Rain on the Pavements* they made the usual attempts to find the person who held the copyright and they came up with a name: Claire Camberton. Could this be the child mentioned by Douglas Lyne? I was given Claire's details and a meeting was arranged.

A woman with bright eyes, animate but tentative, arrived on my doorstep, dragging a large red case on wheels. She was, as she told me, no stranger to Hackney. She brought reams of documentation, photo-copies of letters, snapshots, books: the fruits of twenty years research. She was astonished to meet another Camberton enthusiast and we were instantly exchanging snippets of information, trying to fit the jigsaw together. Claire was indeed the daughter of Henry Cohen, but not the child of the late marriage. Her story was unexpected and poignant.

'I was born in December 1954. My mother's name was Lilian Joyce Brown. She was from Andover in Hampshire. She lived in London during the war, working as a silver-service waitress at the Savoy. She was three years younger than my father. She died twenty years ago at the age of sixty-four. She was a bit reclusive towards the end of her life and fairly secretive too.'

Lilian Brown was in her late twenties when she met Henry Cohen. She attended one of the evening classes he gave, in short-story writing, at the City Literary Institute in Covent Garden. She was by then working in an office as a qualified bookkeeper/clerk. Lilian, her daughter recalls, was a pretty woman who was frustrated by her lack of formal education. She had a sharp eye for antiques and secondhand books and she haunted street markets.

Very soon an affair was underway: 'Mum liked Jewish men, it was a bit rebellious at the time. My father pursued her and chatted her up. Mum told me, in her rather prim way, that he was very virile.'

They came to an arrangement: Lilian Brown would carry Henry Cohen's child and, after giving birth, hand her over. Cohen's mistress of the moment, a Jewish woman, couldn't have children and they wanted to adopt a child. Claire's mother was living in Thornton Street on the Stockwell-Brixton border, and she received an allowance of £26 a month from Cohen's solicitors. She changed her name by deed poll to Camberton. The Camberton pseudonym had a simple explanation. 'My father made the name up by combining Camberwell and Brixton. He hated coming south of the river.' The artist Theo Ramos, who knew Henry very well at the time, has a different story. He suggests Roland

Camberton was an amalgam of Leslie Periton (Henry's accountant and mentor), Ronald Colman (a film star greatly admired by Henry) and Camberwell.

Lilian decided to keep the baby. A terrible scene ensued, the last time the infant Claire saw her father. 'It was all Hollywood then. Everything was a story, a romance.' The estranged couple met on Clapham Common in 1955. 'My father produced a huge stack of legal papers and presented them to my mother. Isn't that dramatic? I was in the pram. That was their final parting, the end of the relationship.'

Scamp presents an anti-hero, Ivan Ginsberg, who courts failure, relishes obscurity, and has an eye for a waitress. 'Ginsberg was very much aware of her desirable presence by his side; so delightful were her little moues and winks that he... felt like... whispering into her ear an invitation.' There was another woman in reserve. 'Until Lolita became his mistress, Ginsberg was delighted with the novelty of this courtship. But afterwards there was nothing to sustain their relations except recrudescent desire... Ginsberg was also still ashamed of Lolita's background, which, though it might supply colour for an adventure, an anecdote, made a long-term affair impossible. At the same time he was ashamed of being ashamed...'

Among Claire's papers was a photocopy of 'Truant Muse', an article by June Rose published in *The Jewish Chronicle* in 1965, just before Camberton died. Rose wanted to discover why certain writers 'whose names were once well known... sped into obscurity.' Henry Cohen, she decided, was 'the kind of individual who finds it pleasant to vegetate.' He retreated to a bungalow beside the sea. 'London history is his special subject and he writes with erudition and clarity in small reviews.' The article is accompanied by a photograph: a balding melancholy man. Like a cinema organist after the coming of sound. Here, without question, is the stalking figure drawn by John Minton for the cover of *Scamp*. That image is taken from life.

And there is one more surprise: a 'major work', never published, *Tango*. The journal of a hitchhiking odyssey around Britain, an English

On the Road. 'The writing is at times Orwellian,' Rose enthuses. Camberton laid out his plans in a letter to *The Jewish Chronicle*. 'My intention is to make two journeys: one, partly on foot, through Europe... and the second to North America.' *Tango* was rejected by his publisher and has not resurfaced.

'Roland Camberton is essentially an isolated figure,' Rose concluded. 'A man in a mackintosh, dignified, anonymous, alone. He is isolated from other writers, from the Jewish community... and his essential anonymity implies almost an element of choice.'

A firm of Wimbledon solicitors informed Claire's mother that Henry Cohen had changed his name a second time, shortly before his marriage. The new name was never to be revealed. The allowance would stop. The site of the grave would remain a secret.

I had been chasing the wrong story. Dying at the age of forty-four, Roland Camberton left behind books that are worth searching out, as well as the lost manuscript of a journey on foot across Europe. At that point in my own life, I had scarcely begun; a Jewish bookseller in Uppingham was considering taking a punt on my first eccentric novel. I had lived in Hackney for twenty years without becoming part of its dream.

Angela Carter

WISE WOMEN

The Chase. That was the name of the road. I remember a basement kitchen. Sitting there, among kites, and painted plates, and cookbooks, with large mugs of tea. Angela Carter was amused, a plosive cackler, swaying and nodding her approval, from somewhere inside an abundance of thick grey hair. I'd come to take away some of the books. She had multiples of *The Infernal Desire Machines of Doctor Hoffman*, and she was happy to sign them at her kitchen table. I was very new, then, to paid publication and had weird assumptions about the relationship between publishers, authors and the backlist.

I first came across Angela Carter, as a poet, in 1963. She achieved a 'recommended' status in a stapled mimeo student magazine published out of Leeds. Her poem was better than that, formally and in substance, ripe with the catalogue of surreal detritus that would make its reappearance in the junkshop of her first novel, *Shadow Dance*, which was published in a shocking pink dustwrapper in 1966. The poem's sophistication is way ahead of the more obvious prizewinners. 'Angela Carter is completely new to us. She is a student at Bristol University. Her letter was funny too.' Bristol, the editors remark, is a hive of potential poets, devouring the ephemeral magazine as soon as it reaches them and hammering out entries for competitions.

Carter, newly married, poses with cat on lap, in rocking chair, for the author photo of *Shadow Dance*. She chose to give up her work as a reporter on a provincial newspaper and moved with her husband to Bristol, where she read English. Bristol was the right place, trading in long-established bohemia, the utopian dreams of Samuel Taylor Coleridge, Robert Southey and the Pantisocrats – and pioneer nitrous oxide gas sniffers like Humphry Davey and Thomas Beddoes at the Pneumatic Institute in Clifton. The geography was right, with the gorge, the wells, the stately terraces. And the social and industrial history of docks, cigarette factory, zoo. Substantial wealth was generated by the slave trade. This was just the kind of place, in later times, for the Blairs to invest in property.

In my discriminate scavenging of South Coast book pits and doggy-damp upstairs chambers in Norwich and private back rooms in Bury St Edmunds, I came upon most of Carter's novels, her stories. I kept examples of all of them and parted with duplicates.

Out of my usual territory, and coming home, after a hunt through the rubbish spread under the flyover at the rough end of Portobello Road, I noticed that Angela Carter and Elaine Feinstein were signing books from a new imprint in a neighbourhood shop. They were launching Next Editions, a stiff-card series, spiral bound, marrying text and illustration. There was a Notting Hill flavour to the enterprise, fired by Emma Tennant, and featuring a selection of her former lovers, including J.G. Ballard and Ted Hughes. And the local sprite, spirit of place, Heathcote Williams. Who was famous for a failed levitation act. And infamous, according to Mike Moorcock, for painting Mike's phone number on walls around the area, after Moorcock broke off his affair with Tennant. She hurled every potted plant given to her by Ballard onto the front path of the property she owned on Blenheim Crescent, where Moorcock rented his overstocked flat.

In her memoir, *Burnt Diaries*, Tennant writes about how, when she was involved with an earlier magazine, she wanted, 'most importantly', to find Angela Carter, whose 'extraordinary, scented prose' she had encountered when browsing in the basement of Better Books in Charing Cross Road. Carter delivers, like musk or some hallucinogenic secretion, the words that Tennant aches to achieve. The two women meet and become friends. There are garden parties, crowded thrashes in a Tennant yard.

'Angela's fascination is so great that it doesn't matter how long one has to wait for the tentatively begun sentence – this broken into by the chisel of high laughter, or the power-drill of an indrawn breath, for she is as amused as any by the kaleidoscope of thought processes which interrupt the consummation of her sentence.'

The interconnections here, through place, patronage, magazines, dinners, meld together some of the best writers of the period: Ballard glances off Angus Wilson, Moorcock seeks out Burroughs and Borges. There is an attempt, before London Overground circuits and orbital motorways, to form a hub, a new vortex; fertile ground where the charting of inner and outer can begin.

Ballard arrives in a white suit and shades carrying maps. 'He is one of those rare beings,' Carter says, 'who talk in grammatically correct sentences.' Emma Tennant, meeting Ted Hughes, thinks of an Easter Island statue. 'I am against my better judgement reminded of Angela (Carter) and her passion for wolves, for hairy men who will suffocate her with their embrace. Has Angela... I wonder... and it comes to me that she said a few months back when I spoke of Hughes's sudden nocturnal visit to my basement kitchen that there had been "something" between them.'

When *Black Venus's Tale*, the book that Carter will be signing in the Notting Hill bookshop, was being solicited by Emma Tennant, the editor took her potential author to lunch at a restaurant called Thompsons. Tennant reports, in her diary, talk of Baudelaire and Jeanne Duval: 'silence filled with half-thoughts'. Philip Roth emerges from the shadows to congratulate Carter on *The Sadeian Woman*. 'Angela's flaming cheeks evincing the mixed feelings a compliment from such a quarter must provoke.'

There was, as yet, no queue in the shop. I was free to mumble my own compliments and to receive an inscription in my book, signed with a characteristic squiggle of wavelets beneath the author's name. Angela was, after all, born in Eastbourne, smelling the English Channel. Her mother, also a mythmaker, said that she had her pregnancy confirmed on the day war was declared.

I met Carter, with the opportunity for a different kind of conversation, at a party for the Guardian Fiction Prize in 1988. She was on an upper level, among excited courtiers and ten-percenters, a silver-maned Gloriana. Beryl Bainbridge, in a little black dress, smoked to something less than essence, clinked on the next perch. So brittle you could flick her with your nail and she would ring like Waterford crystal. They were as necessary to the occasion as the Chance sisters in *Wise Children*. No literary gathering would be complete without one or both.

Angela made a gracious descent into the pit. She really did feel like the godmother for a better class of subversive writing. Through her late novels, I saw our city as a beautiful monster, a mythical being as deformed, heavy-bodied, flighty, vulnerable as her swan-winged *aerialiste* Fevvers. Carter wrote of Michael Moorcock's imagination as 'a vast, uncorseted, sentimental, comic, elegiac salmagundi... so deeply within a certain tradition of English writing, indeed, of English popular culture, that it feels foreign.' She could have been describing herself, books like *Nights at the Circus* and *Wise Children*. Moorcock and Carter, South Londoners both, and world-travellers too, ran the newsreel of history back to music hall, through war traumas and the tricks and feints of bureaucrats and bullies. There was an absolute respect for working lives, an autodidactic love of Shakespeare and the English classics, with no pious whispers in the pews or bowing to established dogma.

Angela made the required visits to W11, but she lived and worked in Clapham. She died too soon, much too soon, to partake of the imposed psychogeography of the Overground. It might have inspired new fictions, stories of Honour Oak Park, Shadwell, Kensal Rise. Her game old ladies, the twin Brixton troopers from *Wise Children*, made play with trams and buses and taxis. On special moonlit nights, they walked. Transport systems incubate different forms of writing; the babble of double-deckers shunting to hospitals, or late-night suburbs, with chemical aggravation. And sudden Jacobean assaults. All the action played out in real time on monitor screens like gallery installations. Trains incline to reverie, Patrick Keiller meditations on housing and decaying industrial stock. The bass telltale throb of a cab pricks sexual fantasy, pre- or post-coital; a sealed off interlude of unearned respite, under the eyes of the voyeur, with his running commentary, as he watches you in the driving mirror.

A taste of what Carter might have brought to the poetry of London Overground can be got from *Nights at the Circus*. Her changeling superstar, Fevvers, buys 'one of those nice big houses off Lavender Hill' for the family. Escaping from a sacrificial encounter with a hellfire occultist, and still naked, she makes her way home from the country. 'Then I went from covert to covert, always concealing myself, until I came to the railway line and borrowed a ride off a load of freight... for I needed the railway to guide me back to London. To my delight, the train soon steamed through Clapham Junction and I nipped out just by Battersea Park, to make my way with all speed through the empty dark up the Queenstown Road ducking behind the privet hedges as I went until I got at last happily home.'

To The Chase. To the home where stories are cooked. To the kitchen table, and the kites, and plates, and retrieved junkshop bits, and photographs. Angela should have, but doesn't need, visible wings. She already possessed the spirit, the energy. The words, when she's on a run, take flight. It's like the technique William Burroughs describes of trying to hit the shutter of a camera at the instant that allows you to photograph the future. You're not freezing anything. You are anticipating a preordained set of circumstances. Preordained, pre-written: found footage of possession.

It was perceptive, and ahead of the game, dowsing the state of early Thatcherite London, the time of the strong woman, to call a novel *Nights at the Circus*. The Thames riverbank would, in a few years, become a circus, with Ferris wheel, chair-lift rides, millennial (discon)tent on the East Greenwich swamps, and a shockheaded mayor as public clown, swinging from wires or falling off a trick bicycle.

After the Guardian Prize affair, the luminaries of the publishing world, the nicotine ghosts, Russian cultural attaché, William Golding, honourable Grub Street irregulars, Angela invited me down to Clapham to buy a few books. That was still my trade, but I was beginning to venture in fiction.

We talked. Even Carter, with her status assured, entrained, at regular intervals, to a job in the creative writing factory in Norwich. She shouldered, I feel sure, more of the grind than was strictly necessary. Her attitude was playful and undeceived about the ultimate value of such exercises: the real writers would write whatever. She gave value for money, listening, encouraging, demonstrating, distributing proper levels of cynicism.

Carter went upstairs to the reserve collection and brought down a bunch of pristine copies of her unsold but desirable stock. It took me time to appreciate that items highly prized by collectors, who had few dealings with the everyday world, meant nothing to the publishing industry. Often a single fanatic could sustain a reputation and keep prices buoyant, as traders scramble to buy from each other, inflating prices, all the way up the food chain.

Then a Norwich friend, the academic and fellow writer, Lorna Sage, arrived. The kitchen conference was unbalanced around the gossip they wanted and the single empty chair. I thought of a phrase of Carter's I'd read in one of the late books: 'the fourth guest at the table.' The absence, the Banquo space that is cousin to Eliot's 'third who always walks beside you.' Mortality. Shadow dance. 'Those who sit in the style of contentment, meaning / Death.'

For my transition, like a slow fade never fully accomplished, from bookdealer to author, Angela Carter was the white witch, invaluable in her support. Providing quotations for dustwrappers. Talking to editors. Writing a substantial piece for the *London Review of Books* on *Downriver*. It launched me by bringing a fresh eye to territory then unfamiliar to most of the scattered literary and academic community.

The essay starts with an ascent from the Underworld, Eurydice in Whitechapel. 'This reviewer is a South Londoner, herself. When I cross the river, the sword that divides me from pleasure and money, I go North. That it, I take the Northern Line "up West", as we say: that is, to the West End. My London consists of all the stations on the Northern Line, but don't think I scare easily... Nothing between Morden and Camden Town holds terror for me.'

Like my earlier film-student self in Brixton, Angela functioned along the black vine of the Underground system, the Northern Line – which suffered from one drawback, fall asleep and you are in High Barnet or Edgware, one of those remote places now supplied by Tesco and Waitrose vans, allowing commuters to order online and never have to venture into a supermarket again. Shopping as a travel accessory.

'To enter, Orpheus-like,' Carter writes at the end of her first novel, 'the shadowed regions of death.' To enter Whitechapel, with its dark history, its toughness, as she comes up out of the tube at Aldgate East on one of her expeditions to Freedom Bookshop in Angel Alley. The bookshop is closed. 'I felt quite the country bumpkin, slow-moving, slow-witted, come in from the pastoral world of Clapham Common, Brockwell Park, Tooting Bec... It was an older London, by far, than mine. I smelled danger... I was scared shitless the first time I went to the East End.'

*

I was invited by the people at the *LRB* for a lunch to celebrate the publication of Angela's piece on *Downriver*, which was that issue's cover story. One of the chapters in *Downriver* was called 'Living in Restaurants'. It was the end of that era, the munching with editors, the scheming with agents, the wild three-bottle promises of publicists, the kiss-off for some television commission. This gathering, four at the table, in a close-packed Italian place, Trattoria Bardigiana, happened alongside Russell Square tube station on 28 February 1991. I know that because Angela inscribed my first edition of *The Magic Toyshop*. At the end of the meal. A slip in her dating of the year gave it a troubling numerology: 19111. Add up the digits, unlucky 13.

'In Britain an enlightened interest in food has always been the mark of the kind of person who uses turns of phrase such as "an enlightened interest in food"... An enthusiasm for the table, the grape, and the stove itself is a characteristic of the deviant sub-section of the British bourgeoisie that has always gone in for the arts,' Carter wrote, in a review that provoked a furious reaction from native piggies. 'Many a serious scholar would consider the reading and creation of fiction a frivolous pastime,' one of them harrumphed.

I wonder if John Lanchester was listening. Before he took an enlightened interest in money markets and the state-of-the-nation London novel, Lanchester enjoyed a great success with *The Debt to Pleasure*. A portrait of a person called Tarquin Winot who progresses quietly around France offering up thoughts on the cuisine, while revealing himself, incrementally, as a monster, a Wilkie Collins villain. Lanchester went on to write foodie pieces for *Esquire*. Back in 1991, he worked as an editor for the *LRB*.

It's likely that all the group at the trattoria table wrote about food, cooking, ethnic experiments; about analysing and describing the stuff they put in their mouths, as they did it, pre-digestion. Restaurant as theatre: a period sidebar, along with creative writing, to the freelance life. Nobody has a divine right to indulgence for inflicting contrived fantasies on the public. But somebody has to produce the necessary chaff for academic institutions to winnow: issues, big themes, novel topographies.

The stuff on the plate was fine. London lunchtime speed service, with tomatoes and curly pasta, as you'd expect, and rich red wine. Did T.S. Eliot pop out from the office around the corner for a morsel of fish? Or did he snap a cream cracker at his desk? If he did not dine, solemnly, at the club. With bishops and bankers. And poets touching him for an advance on their way to Fitzrovia.

I thought about William Burroughs in his strange, submerged years of London exile, checking out mummies, Mayan glyphs and death cultures in the British Museum. I thought about the film *Deathline* (aka *Raw Meat*), in which plague-infested cannibals emerge from the tunnels beneath Russell Square to snack on unlucky tube passengers.

This was not a topic of interest for Susannah Clapp, Carter's editor at the *LRB*, and another former Bristol student. She was next to arrive. She told me that she was working – the project took many years – on a biography of Bruce Chatwin, a slippery subject.

Angela was the last, a flurry of bags, scarf, hair, bus, bad connections from distant Clapham. But she was the star of the show, the Fevvers figure, settling her invisible wings, amused by everything, talking in eloquent bursts and ripples: the representative of what this literary, periodical-producing coterie should be. Head girl.

I hadn't yet adjusted to the idea that somebody would let me publish a book and pay for it. It felt as if I'd nipped out from one of the Bloomsbury hotel book fairs, for a drink and a sandwich, and stumbled on a table of potential signatures. But as Angela talked that new identity settled. It was a job, like any other. The city, London, was the engine. You could feel the beat of it in the simple exchanges of this restaurant, in the tunnels under us. In the old churches and temples of cultural plunder. Writers writing about writers. Walkers colliding and swerving, drawn by the gravity of power in the fossil-crusted stones.

Shortly after this lunch, I heard that Angela Carter was ill, lung cancer. It felt completely wrong. Even the news of it was a physical shock. Recognition had arrived, late, and the work was in flood. The last novel, *Wise Virgins*, lived out, so convincingly, in every creak and jolt, in voice and gesture and bloody-mindedness, the old age in an old city that Angela was never to enjoy. A lovely book that should have flounced off with the Booker. Instead, what is remembered from one of those ceremonies is the episode when the telegenic person who used to be Selina Scott asks Carter who she is and what she does. Which is not so much a criticism of Scott, caught up in action for which she is ill-prepared, but of the notion that prizes, the winning and losing, are a spectator sport fit for an audience who have no intention of reading the books.

For a few months Carter crossed the river to the Royal Brompton Hospital for treatment. She died in February 1992. Lorna Sage wrote the *Guardian* obituary, telling us how 'Angela somehow understood, not just theoretically but sensuously and imaginatively, that we were living with constructs of ourselves, neither false nor true but mythical and alterable.' And she was right about that. As those books live and prove. They inform and inspire our city.

B. Catling

COWBOY (DELETED FILE)

An Oxford professor, the acting head of a respected school of drawing and fine art, a man who had written and published a number of minimalist texts and critical responses to peer group contemporaries, woke early one August morning to find himself overwhelmed by an avalanche of superfluous words. Oracular voices. Nerve impulses that set his fingers twitching with involuntary movement across the keyboard. Like one of his own mechanical sculptures. Call it genius or affliction. The Others were making a communication.

He drank a little, it went with the job. And with the journeys he had to make, between Oxford and London; meetings, conferences, museums, performances. Nocturnal returns. Earlier wives and children in older parts of the town, on the other side of the river, required his attendance. But that was not it. Not the means or the motivation. He rode on coaches, but never buses. In town he relied on taxis, or walked between appointments remembering the days when he cycled from the Old Kent Road to Kensington. Like Malcolm Lowry, this man did not drive: too risky. But he was quite prepared for nautical adventures and owned several small boats. William Burroughs was not a driver anyone would trust. In Kansas, he tried a bicycle, once, with disastrous consequences, looking out for town characters, the Peppermint Man and the Tractor Dwarf. Then a car, but his wiring was all wrong and he was soon persuaded, by the boys in white T-shirts, to revert to passenger status, cane across knees, devouring the action.

Let us give this established professor, who was more than sixty years old when the seizure occurred, the fictional *nom de guerre* of Catling. It's a good name, chiming with cluster-barrelled machine guns and the sacred, sharp-clawed familiars of lost American scribes.

The first book – you could hardly call it a novel – ran to more than five hundred pages before its transcriber drew breath. The author, given his Oxford exile and his enthusiasm for the text, had something in mind along the lines of the poet John Fuller's novella *Flying to Nowhere*. A haunting tale of monks and islands. *The Vorrh*, as Catling called his epic seizure, wrenched all that into visionary delirium; a plague dance of inspired prose lurching and spewing through an Africa of the mind; a humid, reeking interior of cruel daguerreotype imagery, seeded at several removes from Raymond Roussel. Bakelite aliens spoke. Humans stiffened into mummy cases. Slavers were enslaved by the forest. There were savage couplings, tortures, executions: they were delivered with preternatural tact and convulsive humour. The whole extraordinary stew had the same conviction of authority – *where does it come from?* – that Lowry achieved by working and reworking, loading every rift with echoes, drinking to drown the spark, tracking every bead of cold sweat as it ran down his neck and dripped on a tin table. Catling reached this point with no self-reference or self-interrogation, no autobiographical apologies and revisions. He conjured the entire magic lantern show from a single image that haunted him for years: a bow made from a human spine; while his life, as academic and artist, husband and father, unspooled in the quiet disciple of the limestone city.

This was only the beginning. The sequence, delivered with the page-turning impetus of a sensationalist serial of bat women, sewer rats, Spring-Heel'd Jacks, ran to three substantial volumes. My printer shuddered and steamed as it laboured to keep pace with the pages transmitted from Oxford. Catling had produced, in a few months, rising early, sitting in bed, pounding his laptop, more work than I had achieved in ten years. The texture had the power of diction that marks the real thing: it was both pre-literate, in the ordinary way, and post-literate, mutilating spelling, forging new and necessary terms, and making the sympathetic reader nervous: *will I come out of this alive?* Africa infiltrates London: Bedlam, Whitechapel, Thames sediment. The final move to the Estuary, the Isles of Grain and Sheppey, recalls the drunken spree of William Hogarth and Catling's own yarns about his own mysterious origin.

Punch-drunk, dry mouthed, hallucinating, I crawled to shore at the end of the three volumes, with the certain knowledge that the professor hadn't written them. He'd dug them up on the foreshore. From the place where he buried them, centuries before. Like the molten ball of The Stumbling Block, *the terrifying Heneage Street text that he'd melted in a ladle and poured into the Thames, from slippery steps beside London Bridge.*

But the reason I arranged to meet Catling in Dorchester-on-Thames, an English *Midsomer Murders* village where he had set a recent absurdist ghost story (as well as making a memorial cross for the Abbey), had nothing to do with *The Vorrh*. A breakfast conversation was arranged so that I could ask about the sequence that followed that first convulsive spasm. Like Kafka, Catling re-invented *Amerika*: a country more bizarre, and therefore much saner, than the other, the land of Trump and Schwarzenegger and random high school massacres. In the honourable tradition of numerous populists and library cowboys of the southern suburbs – Norwood, Norbury, Croydon – he delivered a rash of western novels. And without feeling the slightest compunction to ride the range or raft down rapids. Michael Moorcock, the pick of the breed, started in short-pants frontier fiction, Kit Carson comics, and Red Indian lore for the *Buffalo Bill Annual* – but the myth caught up in the end, with his migration to Texas. (Where my own papers, drafts, scripts and false starts, were now in cold store at the Harry Ransom Humanities Research Center in Austin).

Why should Norbury connect with the Texas Panhandle? Or Streatham with Sonora? Burroughs, to his own satisfaction, arrived at an explanation for the obligation to write: violation, guilt. Lowry, more painfully than Catling, fulfilled a duty put upon him in some remote karmic existence. He bummed around Yeatsian gyres soliciting coincidences, signs and symbols. Was there a moment confirming the Faustian contract, the gift, the curse? Margerie Bonner, his second wife, fresh from the saddle as a performer in B-movie Westerns, tried to teach him the geometry of the stars (celestial and Beverly Hills). Their meeting at the intersection of Western and Hollywood Boulevard has the force of fable: he arrives by bus, she comes by car (being with Lowry will end all that). She waits at the bench by the bus stop, he steps down. They embrace. They hold each other. They stay, motionless, until Jack King, Margerie's former lover, who has been detained by business, arrives.

'The living,' Yeats wrote in *A Vision*, 'can assist the imagination of the dead.' Lowry, flying back to Mexico from Vancouver, by way of Los Angeles, in 1945, drowsy with booze and pills, living and reliving for fictive remembrance (or exorcism), *Dark as the Grave wherein my Friend is Laid*, says that he has 'only glanced at' the Yeats text. He senses, the desert of Arizona beneath him, 'an organic turning of oneself inside out, the setting to work of all the headlong down-driving machinery of a colossal lethiferous debauch.'

Reality comes close: derangement, skin splitting, bones worn on the outside. Malcolm's crack up. Outside animals revealed by lack of drink. Coffee, undrunk, tasting like mescal. Antabuse. Hideous therapy of suburban London asylums. Denied water, he is doped, fed salt. Rage of thirst. Until he sucks and swallows with bleeding gums from his chamber pot. Until the benevolent, complacent, fat-whiskered medical man brings a bottle of whisky like a telescope filled with urine. Until he agrees that they can cut out a fistula from his brain, carve the bolus, the vegetal core, eliminate the worm. *Word falling*. He can't put pen to the contract. He's shaking too much. He writes standing up, until blue veins harden in his legs. Margerie holds his hand, guides his wrist. The Sussex culmination of a Hollywood embrace: she writes his books. Margerie brings a novel out from the grave. He has written his Mexican friend, drinking buddy of the bad places, back from death.

'Now that *Will* and *Body of Fate* are one, *Creative Mind* and *Mask* are one also, we are no longer four but two; and life, the balance reached, becomes an act of contemplation.'

On 24 October 1917, four days after her marriage to Yeats, Georgie Hyde-Lees began the process of automatic writing. She was conduit and collaborator. 'What came in disjointed sentences, in almost illegible writing, was so exciting,' Yeats wrote. The arousal was nakedly sexual, as was the language that described it. Their marriage partnership was founded on the need to piece together broken fragments. 'We have come to give you metaphors for poetry.'

The honeymoon cottage in the Ashdown Forest in Sussex was in reality a large double-fronted limestone house with views across heathland and the Weald. The drama was played out between Yeats, Georgie, and the untouchable Iseult Gonne (who would elope with the poet and gambler Francis Stuart). All their bad journeys reduced to the dregs of the final bottle, Margerie Bonner brought Lowry to Sussex to die. He could no longer write or lift a glass or stand without support. The books that appeared under his name, having been mangled and scribbled over until they were almost erased, were edited and improved by the survivor, his wife.

Conniption is the word Lowry repeats, as a chant to keep the plane in the air, as he heads to another border crossing and all the waiting ghosts and policemen. 'Consulates. Customs. Conniption all over again. Double conniption. Bribery and conniption. Treble conniption. It is going into hell.' Conniption is hysterical excitement or anger.

There is not one trace of awkwardness in Professor Catling's initiation by Seshat, the Egyptian goddess of writing. He was taken, a little, by surprise. But he was prepared and ready when the moment came. As he was for the overdue award of a medallion from the Royal Academy. The four western novels germinated in a pre-visioned scene that waited for decades to make it on to the page. A tempest. A camp of wreckers and corpse cannibals, outlaws beyond outlaws, in burrows and caves. A ship smashed by the waves. A man who is a woman crucified to a spar. And then the classic trek over the mountains to the settlement where gunmen and surgeons are found. A quest. Snow. The only transport pulled by dogs.

Catling's Amerika is the west of Lewis and Clark, of Cabeza de Vaca. It negotiates with the fabulous, it erupts into skull-stripping violence. There are shacks where men drink, otherwise the land is immense and unknowable. Outside animals are creatures of the earth gods. The writer is not making a report from a foreign continent. He does not draw on cinema and not much on literature. A paperback copy of Cormac McCarthy's *Blood Meridian* that fell into his hands acted as a goad. Not just the bowie knives, the satanic dissent, the Melvillean madness, but a point of technique: narrative would be redundant if the action was summarised, as some of the Victorians did, as the head of the chapter. In truth, narrative would never be a problem, the four novels ripped along like spaghetti westerns, pretty much turning the page for you, as one outrage followed another, one crunch of physical comedy cutting hard against mountains of metaphor. The old photographs burnt like brands.

Like Sergio Leone and Clint Eastwood, Catling found his America in Spain, in Andalusia. The professor takes a winter break from his academic duties. The endless paper-shuffling meetings and convocations of well-dined men in panelled Oxford halls taught him how to detach, how to summon wanted posters of frontier faces, wolf men of the north, muleskinners and sheep rapists, loggers hanging on to rafts, elephants electrocuted in acts of obscene public theatre by Thomas Edison. Catling stared over the heads of the pen-clicking mandarins at a dim oil painting, some college trophy dying, unloved, into its varnish. The formal garden became a set. Figures infiltrated the shadows; they moved and brought him fresh pages for books still to be written. He rose earlier and earlier to accept this dictation.

With Sarah Simblet, a fine artist and gardener, Catling drives into the mountains. Or, she drives. He sits drinking the sharp light, the thinning air, as they climb towards the snowline. They will stay with a friend, an architect. This man suspects, as I do, that there are prose books waiting to be written. He lends the professor a copy of *True Grit* by Charles Portis. Catling has always taken John Wayne, as the Cyclopean bounty hunter Rooster Cogburn, for a role model. When asked how long he intended to continue as a performance artist, he replied that like Cogburn he'd roll on until they had to tie him to the horse.

He sat on a balcony and swallowed the slim book at one gulp. His wife is out, moving among olive groves, a slender, golden-haired figure out of *Alice in Wonderland*. She is gathering almonds to make ink for her drawings.

The Cogburn of the novel is not John Wayne. As Donna Tartt wrote when she introduced a reprint: 'Rooster is somewhat younger, in his late forties: a fat, one-eyed character with walrus moustaches, unwashed, malarial, drunk much of the time.' Cogburn is a veteran of the Confederate Army, one of William Clarke Quantrill's notorious border raiders (spectres of *Blood Meridian*). Quantrill sanctioned the psychopathology of the youthful James boys, Frank and Jesse. The darkness in Rooster – unexorcised, never carried to a sweat lodge ceremony – is a massacre, one of the foulest in the history of a war of extremes, that took place in a small Kansas town celebrated as a nest of Abolitionists: Lawrence. The retirement home of William Burroughs. Out of the Vortex come the horsemen of the apocalypse, the rough riders.

Catling opens himself to these stories without leaving Europe. He throws another log on the fire. There is no laptop here. He scratches at his notebook. Weapons become surgical instruments. They will hang an elephant from a steel frame in a fairground: like some pointy white dunce's cap auto-da-fé of Ku Klux Klan Inquisition penitents. A

Mexican Day of the Dead rioting and stinking with excitement through Coney Island. They will tumble down icy rivers of no return. And hack meteorites out of Greenland.

'I am all the characters,' Catling said. He is Doc Holliday in his dying reverie. He is Holliday's loving whore-mistress. He is not Victor Mature in *My Darling Clementine*. No irony, no nostalgia. Projection. Dissolution. 'I am *all* the characters.'

After I'd finished reading *Cochise Hotel* – as swiftly at Catling absorbed *True Grit* – he sent me a revised coda. 'They were buried the same afternoon in separate cemeteries. Nobody asked why.' The words came back to me when I searched out the graves of Malcolm Lowry and Margerie Bonner in the sleepy Sussex village of Ripe.

Now the file boxes of Catling's novels, in draft, are piled to the ceiling of my room, like coffins after the affair at the OK Corral. Frontier folk, those early settlers, liked to photograph their dead in vertical positions, as if they were still standing, and ready to walk out of the graves, dressed in their best outfits. Once the door is opened, there is no going back. The contract extends beyond author to reader.

'The glass negative was the removal of that splinter in his soul.' In *The Vorrh*, Catling wrote about the death of the photographer Eadweard Muybridge. 'When somebody finally summoned the courage to ask him the purpose of the huge holes he had made, he replied, "I am making a scale model of the Great Lakes of North America."'

Joseph Conrad

THE SECRET AGENT (1907)

The city shimmers, traffic moves a little more slowly, but it was never fast. The clients of the 30 bus out of Dalston Junction are no stranger than they ever were: an excitable young man smoking dope, two women talking fast and loud in Spanish on a shared mobile-phone, a very local youth proclaiming a sudden interest in voodoo. 'You find a piece of gold, bruv, an' you kill your mum and dad. It's interesting, bruv. It's powerful. Africa is powerful, bruv.' Noise levels drop as a sallow, bearded man in an unexpectedly good suit, white shirt, no tie, wrestles with a cumbersome black rucksack. He struggles to extract something and we all struggle with him: designer dark glasses. Now he looks more than ever like a movie assassin. He returns to the bag. Three upper-deck passengers make for the stairs. 'Allo, mum. It's me.' One week on and Hackney transport is the performance art it always was, but more so. The audience is sharper, more alert, quicker to respond.

We have these pictures lodged in our heads. Peeled faces, wet tissue, syrupy blisters: tactful but inadequate masks of surgical gauze. Overripe colour exposed to the forensic intimacy of digital interrogation. A pack of identity card portraits revamped by Francis Bacon.

The ruins we remember from another era – shells of churches, despoiled libraries – survive in romantic monochrome: the comforting lie. Stoic architecture, chippy humans, the Queen Mother like a Pearly Queen visiting the East End. Tumbled masonry, wrecked teeth. War photographers pick their way through the rubble of the new morning making art, framing statuary against a lowering sky.

Now the horror comes in the muted register of the universal mobile-phone greeting. I'M FINE RU OK is the text we receive before we know anything is wrong. Fast-twitch technology anticipates disaster. The latest gizmos mediate between the ugly truth of the streets – dirt, danger, noise – and the CGI cyberspace of the world as it ought to be: blue water, green trees, Barratt homes. Contemporary ruins are never quite finished: shamed vanity project hospitals, state-of-the-art pools that don't actually open. Landfill mountains and dereliction are hidden from the innocent gaze of rail passengers and Olympic commissioners heading eastwards from Fenchurch Street towards Southend. A bright new wooden fence has been erected, miles of it, to cancel blight: the Great Wall of Rainham. Then, suddenly, from nowhere, news reports blow such feeble strategies apart, presenting us, in unforgiving full colour CU, with real damage, actual bodily harm.

We shouldn't, unless we work in hospitals, in casualty departments, witness such things: cooked flesh pitted with dirt, second-degree burns, hands in plastic bags. This, as we eat or slump in our homes after the daily battle with an overstretched transport system, is news from elsewhere. But that elsewhere is strangely familiar. We've grown used to out-of-synch vid-phone quiver from deserts, shanty towns, wrecked tourist hotels. Such sights do not belong in Aldgate East, Tavistock Square. They hurt.

The victims speak with our own voices. They make sense of trauma, placing it in a framework of everyday concerns. Interviewed, the walking wounded fix on certain details; the insensitivity of being led back from the smoke-filled, wrecked carriage past the bodies of the dead. This, they acknowledge, is the Theatre of the City. It is democratic, anyone can join in. The writer Derek Raymond used to call it the 'general contract'. Mortality. Shit happens. You don't have to fill in an application.

We have been told, but we didn't believe it coming from that source, the politicians, that there were people out there who didn't know us but who wanted to kill us. Blow us apart. Destroy the idea of the city as a community, a viable organic entity. They wanted, above all else, to activate one strand of urban life: paranoia. The dark thing that is always beside us, nudged by every 20-minute hold in an Underground tunnel: close heat, no voice, or the voice of some distant robot.

Fear is intensified by devices created for our protection, the 'ring of steel' around the old financial centre, the City of London. If there are red-and-white barriers, checkpoints, glass kiosks, there must be danger. So we suppress conditioned reflexes, we learn to sleepwalk. The money men, the hedge-fund operatives, are not so easily cowed. The events of the morning of 7 July 2005 shifted the climate of investment, risk-takers made their plays. The markets, as Lord Archer repeated time after time in the days when he did the interviews, bounce back. Random acts of terror are finite, the money wheel never stops turning.

We have one further step to take, the recognition that anxiety is now a permanent and irreversible condition. It will happen again and again. We live in a war state, in a time of war. Globalisation makes that possible. Nations are irrelevant. The Americans franchise kidnapping, interrogation. Torture procedures are 'outsourced' to Egypt, Saudi Arabia – even Syria. Just as this London event might well have been outsourced by a fundamentalist brand to local mercenaries, people who look just like us: confused, preoccupied, sweating. Fiddling with luggage, fumbling for tickets.

I used to work on Liverpool Street station at night, humping mailbags on and off trains, at the time of the IRA threat in the seventies. We were told, often, about parcel bombs. Stay alert. Alert to what? The alien with the rucksack? The tourist? Your fellow labourers, that bunch of many-languaged freelancers with the dubious paperwork? Nothing happened, beyond the boredom that is always twinned with terror. The future, J.G. Ballard reckons, is a cocktail of those elements: the ennui of edge-land architecture, airport roads the same everywhere, and highly-visible tanks patrolling the perimeter fence. If an English cricket team ventures to Pakistan it will be accorded, so the relevant diplomat assures us, the highest level of security: 'head of state.' That is to say, public roads in Karachi will be entirely cleared between five-star hotel and stadium. The city of the spectacle is deserted, crowds under curfew, so that the sport of the people can be performed, at a time suitable to the television networks, in a massively guarded redoubt.

The novelty of the recent atrocities lay in the astonishing immediacy of the forms of remembrance. No editing, no staged highlights. No retakes. We seem to be remembering events that have not yet occurred. A fabulous stream of low-definition, drift imagery: pedestrians swimming through smoke and fuzzy light. Recorded by someone, anyone, who is a part of the event, not a privileged outsider. Tunnels and trains captured on a mobile-phone. We see through our pores. We exchange deep memory for a disposable sense of present time. Everything is out there, nothing is special. The past is redundant.

Bomb outrages, or the recasting of such interventions, have been with us for a very long time. Joseph Conrad in *The Secret Agent* (1907) drew on a real-life episode, an anarchist who detonated himself while plotting an attack on the Greenwich Observatory. A simple-minded boy is blown apart by his own explosive device. The planner vanishes into the obscure cinema of the city. 'Nobody looked at him. He passed on unsuspected and deadly, like a pest in the street full of men.' Alfred Hitchcock, translating Conrad's novel (keeping the virus alive), called his 1936 film *Sabotage*. He confessed that it was one of the worst mistakes of his career, the subverting of the rules of suspense, when he allowed the bomb to go off, accidentally, in a London bus.

Now we have a new cinema, requiring minimal light, no technical expertise (switch on and hold above your head like a torch). The people's cinema of the mobile-phone: careless and magical. The results are more precious than the over-considered banalities of picture-postcard television. Those screaming reds, blue bus seats in surreal positions, that potent sign on the cracked destination plate, HACKNEY WICK : we want to avert our eyes.

Mobile-phone reports are unauthored, without ego: the city as itself. At the moment of crisis, phones shift from being mere tools of convenience. They begin to create a poetry of unease. The authorities want you to send in all your digital improvisations, your snapshots, your small vanities: 'I'm on the 30, I'm coming home.' There are specialists in futurology who will examine, like a dubious Old Master, every centimetre of your miniature epic. The explosive devices may well have been triggered by mobile-phone alarms, before the network failed, overwhelmed by its sudden popularity. When we called up that terrible silence.

It might once have been thought that London was a city entirely occupied by dogs and cats. Their humble portraits are stapled to suburban trees, pasted on electrical junction boxes. Rewards are offered for vanished pets. Now human faces, lifted from home movies, nights out, degree ceremonies, replace the animals: proud smiles and troubled frowns. These are the ones who disappeared underground; the children, parents, lovers. They look, all too quickly, faces left out in the weather, like those oval photographs set on gravestones.

Friends email from other countries, the bombs have made news in America. It is the sort of news they understand. A painter who left London for a quieter life on the south coast tells me that she felt, at once, how much she wanted to be back, at home. She invoked the 'spirit of the Blitz', the belief that London was a sentient being. A being she needed to touch, embrace. She reasserted, in her marine exile, a nagging sense of belonging to the place where she had grown up. Trauma sharpened the appetite.

The city writes its own script. Things are always much stranger than they seem. A couple of months ago, I walked around all the London mainline stations in a day, to find what was left of the First World

War memorials, the names of the thousands of railwaymen who died in the conflict. Among the manifold building works that we endure as the cost of our brilliant future are tattered flyers for victims of the tsunami. The King's Cross disaster from 18 November 1987, when thirty-one people were killed, during or after a fire at the station, was presently without any form of memorial. Nobody at the information booth could remember such a remote event. The plaque had been removed, because of building works, to the railway museum in Acton.

The driver of the 30 bus, so I was told, began to walk west, in the aftershock of the explosion, still covered in blood. He walked for seven miles, through the hallucination of London, deaf to the sound of the city, until he found himself in Acton. Geography was confused. His bus shouldn't have been in Tavistock Square. It had been diverted. Only walking, entering the dream, could repair the hurt.

Arthur Conan Doyle

A STUDY IN SCARLET (1887)

All art is at once surface and symbol.
Those who go beneath the surface do so at their peril.
Those who read the symbol do so at their peril
— Oscar Wilde, *The Picture of Dorian Gray*

In the world of fly-by-night publications in gaudy pictorial wrappers, significant events all too frequently pass unnoticed. There is a symbiotic relationship between over-dramatized 'true crime' reportage and transient works of fiction. Without the intervention of an investigator of genius, the murder of a foreigner (the member of an outlandish, polygamous sect) in an 'ill-omened and minatory' house, off the Brixton Road, would seem to belong in the pages of the yellow press. On railway station book racks, shilling shockers are distinguished from the sensational journalism that inspired them only by their price.

In Southsea, a moonlighting oculist with an empty waiting room, a man with time to soak up all the criminous fiction on which he can lay his hands, takes his first shot at penning a lurid shocker. 'The plot thickens,' he writes. 'I began to smell a rat.' He doesn't sweat over this magazine fodder, as he would over one of his serious historical romances. He wraps the business up: hawk-nosed detective and bumbling sidekick, comic Scotland Yard functionaries, a killing on the wrong side of the river, capture of criminal. Done and dusted in a brisk eighty pages. He is then faced with stretching this short story into a saleable novella. The disappointed medical man was new to the game, so he folded in a Western yarn, padded out with purple landscape passages, melodramatic villains and a lachrymose sentimentality that would have embarrassed John Ford at his most Irish.

The working title, *A Tangled Skein*, was a clunker. But it would have to do, while the putative Edgar Allan Poe niggled at his plot. Ormond Sacker, a retired military surgeon, back from a skirmish on the North-West Frontier, relates the adventures of a consulting detective with a surname borrowed from a Harvard professor of anatomy and physiology, the author of many volumes of popular light verse: Oliver Wendell Holmes. Add a preposterous Christian name and the readership for mystery fiction would be introduced to: Mr Sherrinford Holmes.

The author of this fiasco, according to Michael Dibdin in his first novel (*The Last Sherlock Holmes Story*, 1978 – a pitting of the Victorian detective against Jack the Ripper), was always 'getting the dates wrong, falling over the facts, confusing the names.' Editors, to whom the struggling general practitioner submitted his manuscript, were cautious or unenthusiastic. The novella was turned down by the *Cornhill Magazine*, as well as by publishers Warne and Arrowsmith. Eventually, Ward, Lock & Co. agreed to issue it as part of *Beeton's Christmas Annual* in November 1887. By that time, Arthur Conan Doyle had fixed on a new title, *A Study in Scarlet*, and more considered names for his protagonists: Doctor John H. Watson and Sherlock Holmes. Out of such unpromising beginnings, out of financial necessity, boredom, a hungry perusal of earlier models, emerged a book and a set of characters who were to remain as much a part of the fabric of London as the street in which they lived. Their fictitious address, established in the heritage catalogue, took its place alongside Winston Churchill's wartime command bunker, the Tower of London, and the waxworks of

Madame Tussaud.

Holmes and Watson were instant immortals, springing, full-grown and two-thirds formed, from the author's head. It was impossible to believe that they had not always been there: the same age, the same clothes, the same room. The pattern of words on the page was, immediately, so familiar that *A Study in Scarlet*, like *Hamlet*, seemed to be a work written entirely in quotations. Conan Doyle was taking down a form of dictation, accessing voices from a parallel universe (where they had always been present). He achieved, at his first attempt, the absolute feat in the creation of character: he wrote himself out. Holmes and Watson are unauthored. There are stories, Watson refers to them, cases that cannot be told: 'The Giant Rat of Sumatra', 'The Adventure of the Sussex Vampire'.

The public understood, they responded in a way that publishers (who inevitably get these things wrong) failed to do. They understood that 'Arthur Conan Doyle' was a front, a smokescreen, the facilitator of these extraordinary adventures. A hierarchy was very soon established: Dr Watson as scribe, Holmes as true author, working his friend like a ventriloquist, amazing and intriguing him – with Conan Doyle as no more than Watson's literary agent. The lowest of the low. A grubber. A man of business.

Publication of *A Study in Scarlet*, one year before the Whitechapel Ripper murders, was an event of some consequence. Conan Doyle had landed himself with a golem, an unwanted champion who would dominate the rest of his life; a creature who couldn't be killed off (despite his plunge, wrapped in the arms of his dark contrary, Professor Moriarty, into the Reichenbach Falls).

If the plotting and construction of *A Study in Scarlet* are undistinguished, the characterization is inspired. The sense of pace and urgency, nervous rushes across a London terrain that was still relatively unknown to the author, coupled with the establishment of a base at 221B Baker Street, was masterly. The damaged narrator who is convalescing, after receiving a 'Jezail bullet' in the shoulder, during the second Afghan campaign, drifts without purpose through the city.

'I naturally gravitated to London, that great cesspool into which all the loungers and idlers of the Empire are irresistibly drained.' Watson, existing on his half-pension, friendless, without connections, is a sun-scorched Xerox of one of Oscar Wilde's late-century exquisites. Boredom is a necessary vice, not the caste mark of a superior being. His life is without content. Trapped within a posthumous narrative, a prehistory that is shaky at best (the Afghan wound shifting, as he recalls it in the course of subsequent Sherlockian adventures, from shoulder to leg to Achilles' tendon), Watson is eager to discover and define himself by infiltrating the seductive shadow-world of the consulting detective. The outsider (a provincial like Conan Doyle) is integrated into the complex 'novel' of the metropolis. A 'marriage' is arranged to the benefit of both parties. They are connected and earthed. Holmes, preternaturally gifted, vain, emotionally repressed, finds the one person 'innocent' enough to do justice to his legend. Newspaper accounts of the crimes he has solved will be fraudulent; propaganda bent, then as now, by 'off-the-record' leaks and briefings. Pedants, close readers, have twitted Conan Doyle for the way he allows Watson to misread Holmes's character. In *A Study in Scarlet* he draws up, like a lovesick parlour maid, a list of his co-tenant's limits. Under 'Knowledge of Literature', he enters 'Nil'. He is astonished to discover that Holmes has never heard of Carlyle. And yet, a new case launched, Holmes is quoting Carlyle, quoting Goethe; rattling away like a cultural blagger auditioning for a radio talk-slot. It's not that the author is careless with his creations. His creations grow away from him, pick up their own momentum, as their narratives are ghosted by the forms and forces of the city. Watson is an unreliable witness, because he is not in possession of all the facts. He works from a memory-landscape that ages with him; nothing is definitively fixed. All confessions are subject to revision.

What hooks the reader from the first sentence of the first story in which Sherlock Holmes appears is the inevitability of the tale told. Plain language that reads like a medical practitioner's case notes. The narrator announces himself and prepares the ground for the introduction of this mysterious other, the loved one; object of fascination, absurdity, excitement. We are presented with a burnt-out case (not yet optioned by Graham Greene). A man, back from the war zone, searching ineffectually for an energy source. Watson is often confused with Conan Doyle: both are sturdy imperialists, budding, sensible romantics, susceptible to a pretty ankle. Both require the invention of a Byronic alter ego, narcissistic, theatrical, through which to enact their darker fantasies. Sherlock Holmes erupts into *A Study in Scarlet* with the shock of poetry outraging well-behaved, conservative prose.

Conan Doyle is an impresario of pantomime effects. Watson, having been shifted rapidly across the landscape of London ('private hotel in the Strand,' Criterion Bar, lunch at the Holborn, hansom cab), finds himself back at his old hospital, Bart's, in the company of his former dresser, Stamford. Holmes is discovered, through dim, smoky light, busking frantically in the style of Stevenson's Dr Jekyll. Doyle's description is virtually a stage direction: 'This was a lofty chamber, lined and cluttered with countless bottles. Broad, low tables were scattered about, which bristled with retorts, test-tubes, and little Bunsen lamps with their blue flickering flames. There was only one student in the room, who was bending over a distant table absorbed in his work.'

Holmes springs or twists or shouts. 'I've found it! I've found it.' Every utterance comes with self-contained exclamation marks. He'll leap from beating a cadaver with a stick to the discovery of 'an infallible test for blood stains,' to crushing Watson's hand in a manly grip. Off-guard, wincing from the pain, the doctor is amazed by Holmes's opening gambit 'You have been in Afghanistan, I perceive?' Absurdist theatre in its purist form.

No Sherlockian investigator, not one of the imitators, copies or off-cuts, all the way down the line from Austin Freeman's Dr Thorndyke to Sexton Blake, has matched the weird immediacy of the original. Holmes is the divided man that the age required: alchemist and rigorous scientific experimenter, furious walker and definitive slacker, athlete and dope fiend. He could, as the mood took him, be Trappist or motormouth. He was at once the anonymous uncoverer of secrets and the egotist who ensures that, through Watson, an approved biography would be scripted and left for posterity. Holmes is forever lurching between incompatible polarities. He tries to ensure his immortality by committing suicide at the height of his fame, and is then persuaded into a comeback. A grand old trouper, he stays on the boards from the age of Henry Irving to the first rattle of Nöel Coward's cocktail-shaker. By the finish, voice is all that's left: a mellifluous Gielgud whisper offering a series of over-rehearsed and under-remembered anecdotes.

The murder, on the dark side of the Thames, the word *rache* scrawled in blood on the wall of a deserted house, the footprints in the mud; all these tropes, bad weather/sick city, are conjured by Holmes so that he can demonstrate his astonishing skills. Great detectives contrive their own microclimates. Like quest heroes of old, they invent the crimes that test and prove their claims of omniscience. Without the lowlife iniquities of the Brixton Road, there can be no safe domestic enclosure in Baker Street. Without malignant darkness and yellow fog, there is no fire in the hearth, no soft glow of lamplight.

When Holmes is incapacitated by ennui, indulging in his 'seven-per-cent solution', he wills a crime, terrible enough to excite him, out of the ether. A crumpled body in a locked room. A coded message on the table. A league of red-headed men. Then he comes to life and London comes to life with him. Awful though the notion might be, the anguish of an unemployed Holmes (echoed and reinforced by a blocked author who admits that he finds it unendurable to cobble together another plot) is part of a cultural psychosis that finds its resolution in the late century's most brutal sequence of sacrifices, the Jack the Ripper murders. Only after these lurid brutalities can the public be roused from their inertia and made to address the social problems of prostitution, appalling housing conditions, squalor and destitution of the East End.

Holmes affects us so deeply because he is both of his time and out of it. *A Study in Scarlet* (1887) was one of a number of popular books, genre fiction, some of it published in wrappers, creating the myths by which the late-Victorian period can still be accessed. These works are prophetic; through them we can see what will happen, what must happen. Speculative scenarios run ahead of mundane facts: political and social reality is always secondhand. It has been explored and exploited, road-tested by imaginative authors operating in those zones that are only acknowledged by compendium reviews in the humblest corners of the broadsheets. With the passage of time, the throwaway leaflet, the pulp paperback, acquires a posthumous gravity. When it is too late to do anything about it, we begin to franchise (and misinterpret) the visions of writers like Arthur Machen, William Hope Hodgson, Philip K. Dick, Michael Moorcock and J.G. Ballard.

The key Victorian fictions overlap, shadow each other, until their lead characters achieve an independent existence: they are part of the perpetual dream of the city. Stevenson's *Strange Case of Dr Jekyll and Mr Hyde* (1886), Fergus Hume's *The Mystery of a Hansom Cab* (1886), Oscar Wilde's *The Picture of Dorian Gray* (1890), M.P. Shiel's *Prince Zaleski* (1895), Bram Stoker's *Dracula* (1897), Richard Marsh's *The Beetle* (1897): very different but interconnected tales, pertinent fables for the end of a century. They live on the cusp, between Newton and Einstein. Heavy with nostalgia for that which is passing (the exhilarating panoramas of Dickens and Wilkie Collins), they offer a blasphemous welcome to the age of Freud, when all their subversive delights will be 'explained' and dishonoured.

Wilde and Conan Doyle dined together, when they were courted by a representative of Lippincott's Magazine, who successfully commissioned *The Picture of Dorian Gray* and *The Sign of Four*. Wilde expressed his admiration for Conan Doyle's *Micah Clarke*. But Conan Doyle, in his turn, had pre-empted Wilde's languid men about town by setting up Holmes and Watson in their cosy bachelor apartment.

'Nowadays,' Wilde wrote, 'all the married men live like bachelors, and all the bachelors like married men.'

The enfeebled Watson, who admits to 'another set of vices when I'm well', has encountered the dark, mercurial Holmes in the lab at Bart's. His future partner offers shares in his 'diggings': a couple of comfortable bedrooms and a single large airy sitting-room on the first floor in Baker Street. Before this lurch into domesticity, and the admission that he would 'prefer having a partner to being alone', Watson's enervated lifestyle would run along quite nicely with Wilde's *fin de siècle* decadence. The fellow dinner guests, Conan Doyle and Wilde, were rehearsing their own forms of urban theatre: Wilde through modulated speeches and artfully staged dialogues and Conan Doyle through melodrama and Grand Guignol shocks, quick-acting poisons, cab chases, Houdini handcuffs, disguises and transvestism.

Dr John Watson, presented in film versions of the legend as a bluff, tweedy, no-nonsense Englishman, a Nigel (Bruce or Stock), doesn't begin that way. He loafs about town, hangs out at the Criterion Bar, picks up 'young Stamford.' He listens, in fascination, to descriptions of Holmes who is, apparently, 'a little queer in his ideas.' Watson, in fact, starts out as if determined to justify his original, deleted name, Ormond Sacker. (Cousin to Leopold von Sacher-Masoch?). Killing the hours when Holmes is out in the streets, chasing his prey, Watson idles with a copy of Henri Murger's *Vie de Boheme*.

No. 221B Baker Street is a bohemian menage. Tobacco kept in Persian slippers, bullet holes in the wall, correspondence transfixed with a dagger, and enough cocaine for a three-hits-a-day habit. (Is this one of the reasons why Holmes sets out to charm and 'seduce' Watson? As a medical man he might have easy access to substances that were not then illicit, but which came with a dubious reputation. Watson was superb cover. A casualty of war on a half-pension. A natural 'straight' who could be persuaded to become scribe and amanuensis to a glittering, nocturnal career. Watson was invented to invent Sherlock Holmes).

Holmes, sawing away on the violin is a boho poser, a Huysmans aesthete. His attitude to the lower orders, coppers who have come up through the ranks, is patronising. A procession of curious folk, emblematic figures representing the theatrical strands of London life, visit Holmes. What, for example, is Watson to make of the 'railway porter in his velveteen uniform'? These hesitant members of an exotic underclass blink into the daylight like the feral witnesses produced at the trial of Oscar Wilde.

Watson is in a relationship with Holmes such as the one to which Wilde alludes in *The Picture of Dorian Gray*: 'More than an acquaintance, less than a friend.' He withdraws to his bedroom, so that Holmes can conduct his interviews in their shared sitting-room. Holmes is like a school-of-Mayhew social analyst, receiving reports of the city: the 'little sallow, rat-faced' policeman, the 'fashionably-dressed' young girl, the 'grey-headed, seedy' fellow who might have been a 'Jew pedlar', the 'slip-shod elderly woman.' Each character flounces on set; trying for a part in one of Conan Doyle's fictions. They fail to tempt Holmes from his chair. His self-regard remains unpricked. He waits for the opportunity to amaze his new flatmate, to earn the compliments that would bring the blood to his cheeks, 'My companion flushed up with pleasure at my words,' Watson tells us, 'and the earnest way in which I uttered them. I had already observed that he was as sensitive to flattery on the score of his art as any girl could be of her beauty.'

What Watson (on Conan Doyle's behalf) has to provide is a framework in which Holmes can demonstrate his genius. At first reading, which was, after all, the only reading for which the story was intended, *A Study in Scarlet* works superbly up to the point where the body is discovered in the deserted house, off the Brixton Road. The long American flashback and the abrupt resolution are unconvincing and melodramatic. The tale is assembled with a breathtaking exhibition of generic promiscuity: mystery, shilling shocker, supernatural, Western and romance. Conan Doyle borrows from all the popular forms and achieves something that is his own. He anticipates the age of the comic book superhero: Holmes has his uniform, his eccentricities, his 'cave'. From his privileged retreat (with tame landlady and sidekick), he raids the energy map of the city. He is capable of shape-shifting. He can vanish for weeks at a time or disappear into Tibet. His identity is elastic. His tricks are electrifying: part Dr Faustus, part Spring-Heel'd Jack. And, as with the multiverse of the comic strip, the Holmes saga exhibits signs of cross-pollination, withdrawals from (or previews of) other archetypal figures and post-literary identities. Giving themselves up to the relativity of the Sherlockian cosmology encourages future Londoners to time-travel, to re-occupy the alleys, highways and suburbs of the past.

From its opening, *A Study in Scarlet*, operates like a coded manuscript. It is uniquely itself, but it also seems to be about something else. Laboured interpretations are the retrospective delight of literary snoops and textual pedants. Like characters in an M.R. James story, we slide a volume from the over-burdened shelves and waste hours, trying to make sense of a perfectly innocent engraving. The cover illustration for the *Beeton's Christmas Annual*, featuring *A Study in Scarlet*, depicts an adept rising from his chair, in terror of some shape in the surrounding darkness, reaching out towards a suspended lamp. On the table in front of him is a selection of paraphernalia that is as much alchemical as scientific. At his feet is a partly rolled sheet of paper. Chapter 7 of *A Study in Scarlet* is entitled 'Light in the Darkness'.

The elements are magical. Holmes is presented as a sort of conjuror, fiddling with retorts, obsessively pursuing obscure and apparently impractical researches. It is no accident that he is discovered in a laboratory at Bart's in Smithfield: one of the oldest and most mysterious quarters of London, part of a Templar enclave. As Joy Hancox points out in *The Byrom Connection* (1992): 'It is clear that there was an hermetic group in Bartholomew Close based around John Dee's kinsman, David.' She goes on to stress the close connection between experiments in speculative philosophy and the hospital.

Holmes, the fictitious consulting detective, an appropriate figure for his era, is in a line of descent from the Elizabethan magus, Dr John Dee.

Alchemy depends upon twin powders, the scarlet and the white. And these are the motifs that Conan Doyle stresses: paper and blood, a sanguinary message scrawled on damp plaster. *A Study in Scarlet* becomes a literal scarlet study, the cell of an alchemist. R. Austin Freeman who, in Dr Thorndyke, created one of the most credible successors to Sherlock Holmes, published the first Thorndyke adventure as *The Red Thumb Mark*.

'Red,' according to Peter Ackroyd, 'is London's colour.' G.K. Chesterton, in *The Napoleon of Notting Hill* (1904), writes that 'The colour is everywhere, even in the ground of the city itself: the bright red layers of oxidized iron in the London clay identified conflagrations which took place almost two thousand years ago.' Conan Doyle's title, his 'study in scarlet', identifies the novel as growing from the topography of London. 'No red-headed clients to vex us with their conundrums.'

When I wrote my first novel, which was in part an investigation of unsolved crimes from the late Victorian period, I read and re-read all the Sherlock Holmes stories. *A Study in Scarlet*, the more I tried to understand its peculiar fascination, struck me as having a twofold nature: first, the unhesitating conviction of a language-window through which it was possible to enter the London of the 1880s – and then, more disturbingly, the realization that the order of words, the names chosen, was prophetic.

The first Sherlock Holmes story is a device by which coming events are foretold. I found, even though I had my title before I started to work my way through Conan Doyle, that I was echoing the master: *White Chappell, Scarlet Tracings*. Had Conan Doyle, in the trance of composition, achieved a pre-vision of the Ripper murders and published them a year ahead of the event? I was indulging a common fantasy. Many writers had taken the obvious step of pitting the great fictional detective against the infamous Whitechapel butcher. Michael Dibdin in *The Last Sherlock Holmes Story* (1978) and Ellery Queen with *A Study in Terror* (1966) were distinguished examples of the genre. Other versions include *The Mycroft Memoranda* (1984) by Ray Walsh and *Sherlock Holmes and Jack the Ripper* (1953) by Gordon Neitzke. John Sladek's *Black Aura* (1974) proposed Doctor Watson as a Ripper suspect.

'In solving a problem of this sort,' said Holmes, 'the grand thing is to be able to go backwards.' And so I believed. The frequently re-issued pages of print that make up any collected edition of *A Study in Scarlet* would do. I treated Conan Doyle's prose as the artist Tom Phillips treated his *A Humument* (1980) project (the doctoring of W.H. Mallock's Victorian novel, *A Human Document*, 1892). I blacked out words until I achieved a sort of planchette message (appropriate to Conan Doyle's later interest in spiritualism and communication with the dead).

Soon the first page of *A Study in Scarlet* looked as if it had been savaged by a prison censor. Strange new phrases were revealed: 'I took my Doctor and Netley through the course prescribed for surgeons... struck the shoulder... shattered the bone and grazed the subclavian artery... fallen into the hands of the murderous... removed to the base hospital.' Here, in my perverse reading, were the key elements of the Ripper crimes as fabled by Joseph Sickert and franchised by Stephen Knight in his book, *The Final Solution* (1976). The royal surgeon, Sir William Withey Gull, and his coachman, John Netley, are launched on their terrible quest. The warning has been made, coded into this populist yarn, a year or so ahead of itself. Life, by this reading, is merely the confirmation of the best fiction.

My connection of Gull, a successful society surgeon and Freemason, with the fiercely agnostic (and unclubbable) Holmes might seem forced; but the morphic resonance is undoubtedly there. In *The World of Sherlock Holmes* (1973), Michael Harrison writes: 'What Sir William Gull had become to the Royal Family... Sherlock Holmes –

even by the mid-Eighties – was well on the way to becoming in the field of protecting the Great from their enemies' malice.' Precisely the act for which Gull fell under suspicion in the case of the Ripper murders.

Using the names of characters to signal hidden qualities has always been a favourite trick for authors. We look with interest therefore at Conan Doyle's 'Mason of Bradford' as a back-reference to a conspiratorial theme. The name of the marginal figure who introduces Holmes to Watson is 'young Stamford' – which was the town, lightly disguised, where my renegade posse of bookdealers find their own grail, the true first edition, in book form, of *A Study in Scarlet*. The legendary variant preceded the appearance in *Beeton's Christmas Annual*. This item, according to the bibliographer, Gaby Goldscheider, is 'a book so scarce that it has yet to be located.'

Conan Doyle, disturbed by his own 'bad' father, Charles Doyle, a failed artist, a mentally unstable drunk, leaves echoes in *A Study in Scarlet* of a thwarted man, revenging himself by scrawling *rache* on the wall with a long fingernail. The name of the second victim, stabbed by Jefferson Hope, is Stangerson (with its anagrammatic echoes of 'stranger son'). And there are more orphans, lost sons, among the index of personnel: the Scotland Yard detective Gregson and, crucially, the rechristened Watson (what son?). Conan Doyle's naming of characters had a ludic aspect. 'Greg', according to Jonathon Green's *Dictionary of Slang*, is an Irish colloquialism for 'tease'. Conan Doyle had Irish blood on both sides of his ancestry.

If my insistence on a system of subliminal coding is a way of 'legitimatizing' the enduring fascination of this awkwardly structured example of late nineteenth-century genre fiction, it is a minor element in what becomes an enduring and evocative way of reading Victorian London. Conan Doyle realizes, right at the start, that his subject is energy, volition: the survival of individual consciousness against the crushing entropy of the city. London was still, just, knowable. Holmes, like a premature psychogeographer, disappears into the map. Crime is the motivation, the motor force that gets him up from his chair. Unlike his Parisian contemporaries, he is no flâneur, he is a purposeful stalker. 'The game's afoot.' Reach for the Bradshaw. Summon a hansom and off into the purlieus, the unvoiced suburbs.

With the idea of stalking, we come on a motif that is very important to Conan Doyle (and to the mythology of London), the figure of the dog – the urban precursor of the hellish beast of Dartmoor, the Baskerville hound. The dog that didn't bark is one of Conan Doyle's best-known effects. Less has been heard of Dr Watson's invisible bull pup. The keeping of this animal is 'confessed' when Watson lists his drawbacks, before he moves in with Holmes. But the phantom beast is never heard from again. His abrupt disappearance is compensated for in a plethora of canine imagery. 'The old hound is best.' 'I am one of the hounds not the wolf.' Holmes, 'coming upon the right scent', is frequently described in metaphors taken from the hunting field. 'I would dog them and follow them.' 'Gregson, Lestrade, and Holmes sprang upon him like so many stag-hounds.'

'Supposing one man wished to dog another through London?' That question frames the entire Sherlockian project. Every story is a chain of watchers and reporters: Conan Doyle ghosting Watson, Watson inventing Holmes, Holmes trying to become the personification of the city's ambiguities and excesses. Insults and oaths have a canine colouring: 'You hound!' Or 'You dog! I have hunted you from Salt Lake City to St Petersburg.' Or: 'Who talks of murdering a mad dog?'

One of the most outlandish episodes in *A Study in Scarlet* is the killing of the dog. Holmes proves his poison-pill thesis by dosing the landlady's conveniently sick terrier. He waits impatiently for results. Nothing happens and he realizes (or hopes) that the animal has been given a placebo. His relief is considerable when the dog obligingly keels over: 'it gave a convulsive shiver in every limb, and lay as rigid and lifeless as if it had been struck by lightning.'

A troubling cameo, but Holmes warns us off. 'It is a mistake,' he says, 'to confound strangeness with mystery.' Established in his Baker

Street set, the consulting detective is ready to deal with whatever mysteries London can invent to confound and charm him. 'Sometimes he spent his day at the chemical laboratory, sometimes in the dissecting-rooms, and occasionally in long walks, which appeared to take him into the lowest portions of the city.' Holmes was shadowing Rimbaud and Verlaine as they detoured through Limehouse and around the newly dug deepwater docks, brooding on future voyages. With his sense of theatre, his eccentric studies, his urban peregrinations, Holmes is the perfect model for the metropolitan poet, the disenfrancised stroller. Watson is pure prose, functional, unfussy, but not quite as dim as he presents himself. The convalescent military surgeon comes, by steady increments, to appreciate the city. It is revealed to him through his travels with Holmes; glimpses from the window of a hansom cab racing towards the site of the latest atrocity. 'We did indeed get a fleeting view of a stretch of the Thames, with the lamps shining upon the broad, silent water; but our cab dashed on, and was soon involved in a labyrinth of streets upon the other side.'

The quest heroes, knight and squire, journey between the familiar clutter of their Baker Street den and the dark wilderness of the city, with its mazy lanes and secret rooms; between memory and forgetfulness, life and death. As they jolt over the cobbles, Holmes recites a litany of place names: 'Wandsworth Road. Priory Road. Larkhill Lane. Stockwell Place. Robert Street. Coldharbour Lane.' Watson, as Conan Doyle's representative, is initiated into the mysteries of place. The particulars of London with its 'mud-coloured clouds' and its 'endless procession of faces' become a phantasmagoric lantern show of all that is still to be written: biographies of 'real life' criminals, such as the poisoner Neill Cream who arrives, like one of Conan Doyle's avengers, from across the Atlantic, to take up residence in South London. 'If he be Mr Hyde, I shall be Mr Seek.' Conan Doyle will have taken to heart those words in his paper-wrapped copy of Stevenson's *Strange Case of Dr Jekyll and Mr Hyde*.

The would-be author indulged in 'voracious and indiscriminate reading' as he waited for the patients who would never arrive in his Southsea surgery. And through his reading, reveries about his time as a medical student in Edinburgh, the inspirational Dr Joseph Bell, there emerged the outline of one of the stories by which the age would be defined. Conan Doyle was conducting a séance with the future, until he was forced to rise from his chair, like the figure drawn on the cover *Beeton's Christmas Annual*, to reach out towards the suspended lamp, to weave a fable from the shadows on the wall.

Patrick Hamilton

CLICK CLICK CLICK:
HANGOVER SQUARE (1941)

Bob the pub waiter in Patrick Hamilton's 1929 novel, *The Midnight Bell*, establishes a pattern the author would follow until the end of his days: rivers of booze, obsessive pursuit of the wrong woman, rapidly diminishing funds, time killed in afternoon cinemas.

Click. A sudden clouding of consciousness, a welcome amnesia taking the edge off the blight of the city. The Hamiltonian beta male, dead-fleshed, bloody of eye, derives from Ford Madox Ford. Fat Fordie, master of style, is wounded, unwelcome in polite society; he dreams of getting back to the country, a small-holding in Kent or Sussex.

Click. George Harvey Bone is the antihero of Hamilton's masterpiece, *Hangover Square*. He fantasises about beating a Mosleyite to death with a golf club, drowning an inconvenient woman, escaping to Maidenhead. The English idyll: a summer picnic on the river with mummy, sister, or motherly first wife.

If those references are too abstruse for a period that suffers from its own cultural blackouts, embargoes on Edwardian novels as films, think of Hamilton's standard male character as an oversized, inconvenient, upstream type: Boris Johnson (the performance, not the canny operator) in pursuit of Natasha Kaplinsky (overbright eyes roaming the set for more profitable company). The man keeps his baggy flannels up with an old school tie. He peeps out from under a thatch of calculatedly unmanaged hair. All of Hamilton's favoured tropes decay in the same fashion, from the figure observed in saloon bar to media Xerox. His favourite plot device, the psycho driving a decent (but dumb) woman mad, is currently being resurrected on *Coronation Street.*

Doomed to be reforgotten, revived, lost again, Patrick Hamilton remains a very local treasure. Even in 1946 he was being discussed by the critic John Hampson as part of 'the underground.' 'Conversations have a likeness-to-life which become frightful since they are nearly always dreary with the banalities of day-to-day existence.'

Hamilton is lined up against the wall with B.L. Coombes, Jim Phelan, Mark Benney – and who, apart from untenured academics and used-book dealers, remembers any of those? Graham Greene, a Hamilton admirer, knew how to play by establishment rules; he understood that the first duty of a writer was to create a mystique, a brand. The career would follow: good club, remedial travel, amateur espionage and professional religion. (Hamilton favoured the Savile Club, only because there were three members rumoured to be bigger drunks than he was).

Greene could afford to patronise Hamilton, calling *The West Pier* 'the finest novel written about Brighton,' only because the canonical status of *Brighton Rock* was secure. John Boulting's film was in the can. (*The West Pier* is not even Hamilton's best book about Brighton. It doesn't achieve the hallucinatory conviction of the seaside excursions in *Hangover Square*: solitary dinners in private hotels, pointless walks, marine melancholy).

The reception for screen versions of Hamilton's plays was lukewarm. It was worse for the filmed novel. The 1944 travesty of *Hangover Square* was considered a fiasco. George Sanders, the second lead, put it about that Laird Cregar, who played Bone and whose pet project it had been, was so upset by the sacrilege that he immediately died of a heart attack.

For Hamilton it was more serious: his first viewing was so painful that he got drunk and made contact with Lady Ursula Chetwynd-Talbot (known as La), the woman who became his second wife. She stayed with him, on and off, to the end: separate bedrooms in a retirement home on the Norfolk coast. La's room had a Yale lock on the inside. Hamilton's pleasures were small: picking up his daily bottle of whisky from the chemist, re-reading Sherlock Holmes and Hopalong Cassidy, and watching pony club girls bounce around a rough field.

Drink and tranquillised sleep. 'There was a fog even in the cinema,' reported Bob, Hamilton's befuddled waiter, when he hid away in the picture palace attached to Madame Tussaud's in Marylebone Road. Earlier, Bob had enjoyed a double-bill in the company of a friendly barmaid (taking his mind off the prostitute he was pursuing): a Richard Dix feature, followed by twenty minutes of Fritz Lang's *Spione*. Like Hitchcock, Hamilton learned how to work those weather metaphors: slush, sodden streets, the yawning parenthesis of the English Channel.

The grammar of film leaked into the novels. Where Céline, describing London, uses ellipses to sustain a centripetal charge, suburbs to centre, Hamilton favours the more leisured dash. He is changing gear, trying for a clean cut. His fiction is more sophisticated, cinematically, than any of the films that derive from it: until Hitchcock makes his singular translation of *Rope* in 1948.

Autobiography, the writing of fiction, the visiting of afternoon cinemas, gradually merge in Hamilton's addiction, his heroic attempt to drink himself to death (a macho pissing contest with Malcolm Lowry, refereed by their puce-cheeked contemporary, John Davenport). 'It's a shame,' said William Faulkner, 'that the only thing a man can do for eight hours is work. He can't make love. He can't drink.'

Hamilton did his best to prove him wrong – and triumphed in the hallucinatory reality of the novels. George Harvey Bone and a troop of fellow-travelling fascists in polo-neck jerseys, car salesmen from Great Portland Street, tarts, actresses, professional bores and road-house bullies are the nightmare extension of the things Hamilton encountered and couldn't erase in a trawl of Fitzrovia pubs and small

South Coast hotels. Desperately invented fictions fill the gaps in the novelist's traumatised memory.

The Hamilton films, which arrived in a cluster in the 1940s, should never be compared with the plays and novels that inspired them. The two versions of *Gaslight*, the English and the American, I remembered as auditions for afternoon television: stagey, fluid (in the case of Cukor), and concentrated around performance. *Rope* was respected as a technical exercise, but it left me, at first viewing, with a sense of claustrophobia, sick skies on an artfully contrived set. Too many actors, too close to the edge of the screen. I missed *Hangover Square* and had to make do with sniffy accounts in Hamilton biographies.

Putting aside the novels and coming back to the films, I saw them with fresh eyes. The key Hamilton terms are missing: *cement, plains, pleasure*. Those three words recur endlessly, as he describes the slate and limestone city of *Twenty Thousand Streets Under the Sky*. Hard, unyielding surfaces. Snot-grey grass. Miserable hotels. Crowded bars. But Hollywood doesn't do cement or pleasure (as Hamilton understood it). It specialises in surface, overblack shadows that follow actors across trembling walls. Angela Lansbury – whose first part, at 17, was playing the pert housemaid in *Gaslight* – says that she didn't see daylight for the length of the shoot.

Thorold Dickinson directed the first version of *Gaslight* in 1940. A respectable British production: busy streets and squares, newspapers rolling off the presses, low-life music halls, an ex-detective out of Wilkie Collins. Here was an effective facsimile of a lost Victorian world: a waxed-moustache melodrama of the sort Hitchcock left behind when he moved to California.

Hollywood bought the property, destroyed prints and hired noted 'woman's director,' George Cukor, to give it class. Charles Boyer climbed on his box and Ingrid Bergman, tactfully photographed by Joseph Ruttenberg, emoted to her Oscar. Cukor's camera glides. Lansbury offers the first demonstration of a malign spirit beneath a pleasantly skewed exterior that would reveal itself, years later, in *The Manchurian Candidate*.

Netta Longdon, in *Hangover Square*, is asked about the kind of man she fancies. 'Oh... Boyer,' she says, with 'a little smile which conveyed a world of wicked and selfish meaning.' But it's not Boyer she gets, not in John Brahm's 1944 desecration of the novel; it's the supremely odd Laird Cregar. It was evidently decided to throw away everything of Hamilton's novel, apart from the psychopathic sexuality, now pulped into the conventions of the shilling shocker.

Brahm's film is a minor classic, a shotgun wedding of expressionism and surrealism: barrel organs, leering pawnbrokers, cor-blimey-guv urchins. Linda Darnell enthusiastically impersonates a knicker-flashing singer with flea-comb eyelashes and hair in which you could lose a nest of squirrels. There are two standout sequences: the expressionist bonfire on which the faithless Netta is incinerated, while a mob of Ensor devils howl and chant – and the surrealist concerto, as Bone hammers away at a blazing grand piano. Bernard Herrmann, Hitchcock's composer of choice, soups up a score that drives the whole nutty phantasmagoria along, like a candlelit pleasure steamer plunging over a frozen waterfall.

The click that Hamilton described so well, an involuntary shift in consciousness, happened to me as I re-watched *Rope*. No other director was as temperamentally suited to take on the job: Hitchcock and Hamilton shared an interest in the methodology of murder, in permafrost blondes, bondage, sadomasochism, fat-boy humour. Hamilton, through his theatrical contacts, was licensed to stalk Paulette Goddard and Geraldine Fitzgerald. Hitchcock invited Bergman, his current fetish, to visit the set of *Rope*. She came with Joseph Cotten (who had played the detective in Cukor's *Gaslight*). Production stills and shots of celebs dropping in on Hitch make up an unreleased graphic novel. Studio portraits look like Weegee mugshots. James Stewart, back from war, is sick of the whole business: the complicated ten-minute takes with sliding walls and electricians in shot; the subject matter, the long days rehearsing camera moves, while the actors get pantomimed silent movie direction.

Hitchcock's private agenda was a De Quincey essay on 'Murder Considered as a Fine Art'. He would toy with an unpleasant homosexual thrill-killing (and expose homosexuality as the crime). Cary Grant and Montgomery Clift, the proposed casting, weren't playing. So Stewart took a substantial chunk of the budget to wear a suit that looked very much like the one in the 1929 production of the play. There is no hint that Stewart's character is gay, or that he has had an affair with one of the killers. Everything is coded in capital letters.

Hamilton found no such way of disguising his demons. Hitchcock enjoyed gourmet meals and conducted script conferences in his Bel Air garden, over bottles of fine wine. Hamilton was drowning in whisky. The cures never took. He followed an apomorphine regime devised by the same Dr Dent who later treated William Burroughs. He suffered seven brain-toasting ECT sessions at Woodside hospital in Muswell Hill. 'That's you done to a nice turn,' said hearty Dr Hobson. Life was now utterly flavourless. Hamilton had lost the taste for previous pleasures: golf, chess, tying up prostitutes. He couldn't write, he couldn't even dictate. He shuffled between increasingly irritated wives.

Click. Cut to black. Flashback to the beginning of *Hangover Square*. 'He turned left... and away from the sea... towards the street that contained the semi-detached villa in which tea, with Christmas cake and cold turkey (in front of an electric fire at eight o'clock), awaited him.' Patrick Hamilton's ashes were scattered over the Blakeney mud flats, within sight of a cold, grey, uninterested ocean.

John Healy

THE GRASS ARENA (1988)

'Suddenly a hand wrenched my neck back. Others grabbed my arms, my legs... One of them squeezed my balls so hard. I got a pain in my guts making me dizzy.' Brooding silences wind the tension to breaking point and are punctuated by sudden eruptions of violence: it is a survivalist world, bleak and uncompromising: the world of competitive chess.

John Healy arrived there, without papers or proof of identity, a drowning man coming up for the last time. It was his only way of escaping from the slow-motion suicide of alcoholism, and he took it with manic relish. *The Grass Arena* is a devastating account, told directly and without subterfuge, of that journey. Painfully retrieved highlights stun the reader like blows from an invisible assailant. The procession of images once launched seems predestined: savage childhood, petty crime, the Army, booze and vagrancy; a willed renunciation; rebirth into chess, guru-chasing and, inevitably, the in-tray of Colin MacCabe at the British Film Institute.

Now the book (or, more accurately, John Healy himself) is everywhere: the knock-on effect, the metropolitan whispers that can rush the latest hot item from the *Guardian* to the heavyweight Sundays. An authentic report has been brought back from somewhere exotic and unknown, the pavements of this city. And as the gadarene sprint of enterprise capital attempts to corral any citizens with loose change in their pockets into Fort Apache-style ex-industrial ruins, such as the Bow Quarter, so life outside, street life, with all its fevers, is reduced to a matter of local colour, window-dressing, spice to garnish the sales patter. We are acquiescing in a scenario that ensures the success of such a testimony as John Healy's – if only because these things will soon be as scarce as functioning shops on the Isle of Dogs. The miracle is that the book exists at all: it is what we remark on, ignoring the buoyant and quirky humour that makes the grim tale palatable.

The story needs no introduction, it tells itself. Healy's methods are basically conversational, with a narrative drive that is apparent from the first sentence. He does not deserve, or solicit, Colin MacCabe's attempt to marry the 'crippled Utopianisms' of addiction and political terrorism. Nor does he demand, beyond the desirability of a strong quote for the dustwrapper, any comparison with William Burroughs and *Junkie*.

We are told by MacCabe that Healy's reading habits favoured crime fiction. Therefore, it is presumed, he dropped naturally into 'the hard-boiled cadences of a Hammet [sic] detective novel.' In fact, the only time Healy did any reading was in prison. Put away for a few months at a stretch, he found that for the first two weeks he could barely see: it was a physical struggle to unstick his eyelids. Thereafter he binged on the excesses of James Hadley Chase, the thrill technician guilty of *No Orchids for Miss Blandish* and the psychotic charms of *Twelve Chinks and a Woman*.

Healy's style, though it borrows the odd shrug or swagger from twin-fisted romance, is his own. It is the evenly-modulated voice of the yarn-spinner, the spieler: remorseless, unflinching, letting each episode die into its successor. 'My father didn't look like he would harm anyone.' The opening gambit is deceptive, warning us that fists will soon drum against the child's skull. How did he survive? Physically slight, an Irish immigrant with a Londoner's tongue in his mouth, he was belligerent with innocence. He belonged nowhere. His minimal presence in the family home was enough to infuriate his father and bring down the repeated assaults of fate.

The narrative is chronological, its rhythms are swift and terse. There is an overwhelming sense of the authorial presence racing to snare memory beyond memory, without a hint of the self-promoting strategist faking the odds to ensure a final apotheosis. The plot will be familiar to readers of ghosted East End gangster memoirs: bother with the law, church, boxing club, billet in the White Tower. Colchester, battalion champion, guardhouse, on the trot. It is at this point that John Healy's autobiography diverts spectacularly from the route chosen by those premature Thatcherites, the Krays and their cohorts. They plunged into the abyss with their eyes wide open. Pockets pillowed with banknotes.

A natural defaulter, Healy deserted to Ireland, willing an escape into his imagined past. A dream landscape: the world slowed down, physical sensations overwhelmed him. He had infiltrated the pages of Patrick Kavanagh's *Green Fool*, but the lyricism was spattered with ancient brutalities; bedridden bachelors, mud-slow policemen, bicycles, stone fields – and, always, the drink. Attending him on the farm, as in the city, never further than the end of the bed, was his dark twin, 'tension'. A shudder, a shoulder-twitch, a clinging sense of doom that Jack Kerouac called 'The Shadow'. There was the expectation of disaster that made its arrival ever more certain. The shudder can only be muted in black pints, the drinking life, oblivion: clubbing the wolf into silence, inhibiting conditioned reflexes. The slide into vagrancy is a letting go, a surrender that is not without its compensations.

The vagrant in fiction is a solitary with 'a past'. His descent into the nether regions is frequently heroic and, in achieving it, he is ennobled but emasculated. David Goodis is the laureate of this mood. William Kennedy, a more recent mythologist of hobo as artist, has seen his novel *Ironweed* make it all the way to the screen, where Jack Nicholson was obliged to continue his career-long impersonation of the sneering loner. Other avatars range from the rabid peasant-author of Knut Hamsun's *Hunger* to the 'tramps' who enliven the conformist fringes of Richmal Crompton's Arcadian sagas. Another striking manifestation has been the vagrant-spectre who roams the blighted London of Peter Ackroyd's *Hawksmoor*. These drop-outs are all repositories of forgotten knowledge; ageless and fraudulent.

But they remain strangers to Healy's *Grass Arena*. His drinkers belong to established 'schools'. Outsiders, attempting to break into protected circles, would not survive. There are no personal histories beyond tribal knowledge, the tricks of subsistence. These men and women are ruthless in their self-interest, but share the only thing that matters, the bottle. Alone, they would die. They would be picked off in days by a society that has no use for them. They are unexploitable. Their friends will strip any remaining assets if they falter. They will clean out the pockets of the epileptic or the dying. They have their territories and they hold them. They cluster safely within the maternal embrace of the particular railway station that links them to their place of origin: so that the Irish stay on a tired grass patch alongside Euston, where they tumbled from the Liverpool train, white Jocks wander the perimeter of King's Cross, eager to avenge imagined aboriginal slights.

Communication, speech itself, is a dangerous luxury. Sudden bolts of violence climax some rambling monologue, while Pinter playlets are consummated in blood and froth. Healy sketches these dramas with forensic skill: the pivotal moment in the bar when the man beside you decides to shove a broken bottle into your neck. Peripheral vision is an essential tool. The wino's life depends upon a kind of neurasthenic subtlety. All those sentimental low-life icons are torn to shreds – as when the genial tart's salutation sends Healy spinning into a scramble to escape from her black pimps. He is offering us that species of fate-tale perfected by the late Jim Thompson, himself, like so many hard-boiled practitioners, no stranger to the bottle.

The liberal press have tended to receive this book as startling intelligence brought back from some impenetrable other world. It is happening elsewhere. We are, of course, properly concerned but not implicated. It is all as fascinating and remote as a traveller's tale, and as hygienically distanced as Arthur Morrison's *Child of the Jago* or the 'Monster Doss House' photographed for the first edition of Jack London's *The People of the Abyss* in 1903. But the news is that the Doss House is still there in Fieldgate Street, looking ripe to fall to the front-line developers whose eyes light up as they prospect yet another authentic poverty facade. Those wonderfully gothic post-Ripper slums were built to last for a thousand years, a reich of charitable intentions. Beyond them, shadowed on the itchy grass, are the immortals: the unhoused, the 'wet-brained,' the psychopaths.

What might be disturbing, to those who have up to now preferred not to think about it, is a sub-text that Healy lays bare, but does not stress: the way that the state exploits our indifference to demonise these marginal non-producers. There is, as yet, no theme park in which to display them as shudder-inducing Dickensian chimeras. That may come. For the time being we condone, with a nod and a wink, what can only be called a policy of unauthorised culling. Clean-handed collaborators, we are able to mime our horror as each freakish example finds its way onto the inside pages of provincial newspapers. The vagrant is at the bottom of the trench, a social zero. He is loud, aggressive, foul-smelling, incontinent, abusive of authority, eager to lift anything that isn't chained down. Bored coppers, uniformed garbage collectors in unmarked vans, get their retaliation in first, bend the rules of engagement, kick the living daylights out of their conveniently anaesthetised customers, speeding them on their way down hazardous staircases. They ballast their pockets with strips of lead, in order to massage the arrest statistics and shunt the problem onto the overcrowded shambles of a Victorian prison service. The weaker brethren are ticketed for the path labs and we are rid of them. Medical benevolence is restricted to cocktails of Scotch and Antabuse: the obliging guests retch up their intestines, yard by yard. The quacks 'always put "Heart attack" on an alky's death cert.' Who is going to complain? Certainly not John Healy. He has surfaced with enough rancid anecdotes to launch a first novel and two or three plays. He is a writer, and the worse things get the better we like it. But when he strolls through the grass arena, nostalgic for its 'strong energy,' the old faces are missing. The body count is unchanged but other death masks stare at him without any spark of recognition.

The helpless and the hopeless are dumped in the rag shop at Pentonville, a mumbling crew of psychos and inadequates, suffering the casual viciousness of the system, and the spasmodic spankings of the gangsters on top of the rat heap. Healy's twitchy intelligence, his street nous, kept him clear of the worst of it. But he remembers, and will never shake free from, the screams of some feeble-minded sex offender whose eye was skewered on a needle by a quorum of high-minded moralists.

The author is now a lively, but posthumous man. He is a youthful, if slightly foxed, forty-five-year-old. He can scarcely believe that his dream of the past happened. As if to prove its truth, mostly to himself, he heaps verification into your lap: corrected typescripts, and the Junior ABA certificates his mother preserved, along with the chess cuttings from the *Evening Standard* that Faber chose, rather pointedly, to reproduce on the final page of the book, as if to say: 'See, dear reader, it's all true!'

Healy takes your hand and gently guides it towards the hardened tips of his ears, where the frost-bite got him. He balls his fist to model the displaced knuckle. You admire the particular quality of blue in the scar tissue around his left eye. He can no longer dredge up the stories of all the wounds: after the first eight pints there is only darkness. He could have killed without knowing it or fathered children.

The coda, asserting that there is life after alcohol, takes up only twenty-six pages. He knows that half his brain has gone forever, shrivelled by horror. Chess, despite the modest sponsorship of Jim Slater, is not enough. Card-carrying members of a yogic orange lodge tempt Healy to India, where he discovers only heat and confusion: beggars more terrifying than anything in the Cider House. They hustle and bait him, these demons of guilt. Neither is the ashram much help: 'In India we do not sit on holy books.' His dream woman, 'the Countess,' evaporates, another post-traumatic illusion. 'Time clouding memory cured my longings.' The light goes out and the story ends.

Now the jackals, myself among them, beat a path to the door of his mother's flat, tucked away off the Caledonian Road in a labyrinth of brutalist concrete that would astonish that earlier inhabitant, Samuel Beckett's Murphy. A novel, *Streets Above Us*, has been completed, its title joyfully echoing Patrick Hamilton.

It would be a nice irony if the brewers, Whitbread, saw their way to handing John Healy a cheque that would keep him writing for the next year or so. I shall certainly be watching out for whatever emerges – if Healy does not get bored with practising a form he has already mastered, or discover that there are more scoundrels in Bloomsbury than in any *Grass Arena*.

GAUDY LIVING

Nice motor, John. A shiny-bright Mazda in the neon-splash of wintry Belsize Park. Broad pavements and discreetly established shops with their immigrant traces. John Healy, storyteller, ex-wino, ex-vagrant, recidivist, boxer, has invited me for a meal at Chez Nous. Now, out of the air, he slips me a Christmas envelope, a nice little drink. From the inside pocket of his new overcoat. Success, when it hits, is to be shared. There's a film in the offing, loosely based on his only novel, *Streets Above Us*. The underclass underground. Customized retrievals (word-processed by a script doctor) from John's former life as a dip, a handbag ferret working the Green Park-to-Victoria shuttle.

That's the moment, tearing open, with cold hands, John's brown envelope: the moment of fracture. The last time such a thing happened was in dubious, back-of-the-lorry slaughters out in Chobham Farm, Stratford East, in days of my own bourgeois-boho poverty. This street survivor is the only person, in plenty of years, who has picked his own pocket on my behalf.

Healy, as far as the publishing/promotional nexus was concerned, was a revenant who had the bad manners to stick around when the launch party was over. Every lowlife is allowed one book. *The Grass Arena* had been patronized with enough prizes. Why didn't Healy take his yellowing cuttings and fuck off, back where he came from, into nighttown?

So began the second, and far worse, period of internal exile and ostracism. The days of the blacklist after that misunderstanding with the claw-hammer in his publisher's office. Healy had lost the communality of the wet brains and methsmen. The faces were gone and those that were left would make short work of someone who had crossed the road and been invited inside the lighted building. Drink dissolves time. You day is defined by unquenchable thirst. A journey from Euston to Finsbury Park is an expedition to a foreign country. Shift a couple of postal districts and your permissions are deleted.

So John circumnavigated his mother's modest flat, off Caledonian Road, and the chess clubs of Hampstead. He found himself invited, as vagrant of the month, to liberal mansions at the top of the hill. 'Go on through,' they said to him. He was two courses into the banquet before anyone else came into the dining room.

He was meditating, doing the exercises and writing: stories, novels, screenplays. Nobody wanted to know. He had made his pitch and his biography was used up. They remembered that wonderful film with Mark Rylance. The book was redundant. Rylance's impersonation was uncanny. He was more like Healy than John. The thing that really disturbed them was this: if the man was alive and well, chipper as a cricket, cranking out novel after novel, memoir after memoir, then the sentiment they had invested in the original yarn was misplaced. An early death, coughing up his guts, was the least they could expect. The lack of gratitude was staggering. The reviews had been written under false pretences. Those raves were disguised obituaries.

The books drifted out of print. The follow-up to *The Grass Arena*, the second act of a one-act tragedy, went the rounds without a nibble. But now, through the lucky accident of the film money, it could come up camel hair.

I watched the Mazda pull out into the dripping mist. John was on the up. He waved. He told me that he kept a paperback of *The Grass Arena* on the seat beside him. There was no unnecessary paperwork or insurance for his motor, but the book was better than a passport. The old bill would never hassle a man with the status of a published author. And the photo to prove it.

Thomas Holmes

LONDON'S UNDERWORLD (1912)

Thomas Holmes, with his tilted bowler, Wyatt Earp moustache, raised brows, belongs in the Old West: narrowed eyes burning out of a sepia album. A serious person capable of living on both sides of the law. A hard-bitten enforcer of morals. A bounty hunter for truth. Holmes, from what we know of him, his incessant prowling through London's subterranea, strove to be that most difficult thing, a good man in a bad place.

Settling in the suburbs, in Bedford Road, Tottenham, he respects a tradition established by upwardly-mobile police officers, fictional or documented. A short ride or a brisk stroll from the labyrinth, the ghetto, the criminous swamp. Alexander Baron's Inspector Merry from *King Dido* (1969) – a novel written in homage to Arthur Morrison – is a nice example of the type: courteous, dynamic, and on deceptively cosy terms with villains and malcontents. A recognised outsider, Merry enjoys the liberties of the shadow world, but returns, nightly, to his new home, which is to be found in 'an enclave of broad roads and classical villas in the midst of a poorer London.' In somewhere like De Beauvoir Town, on the Islington side of workaday Kingsland Road. Merry 'took a tram to Shoreditch and walked down Bethnal Green Road to the police station.' *King Dido* opens in 1911, the year before

London's Underworld was published.

Thomas Holmes walks, walks, walks. Like Mayhew. Blanchard Jerrold. Thomas De Quincey. Like all the pilgrims, statisticians of poverty, reformers, visionaries fascinated by the machinery of the city, our ever-expanding metropolis. Holmes is always in movement, down among the vagrants and derelicts of the Embankment, steeling himself against the stench of some lodging-house kitchen (burnt sausages, smoke fug, close-packed humanity). He misses nothing: clothes, hair, sallow skin, scuffed boots and bloodshot eyes. Prisons, charity pits, coffee stalls. He is a patron of London's invisibles; an undeceived listener to improbable and self-serving fictions. And, like all the other stalkers of the shallows, he is also a writer. Extinguished hopes, submerged districts, become the material of his direct and masculine prose. He will describe the horror, shame and degradation of lives endured at the limits of the possible. He will factor anecdotes, trade in the picaresque. The better to engage your attention, to pick your pocket (in a good cause). And he will find solutions. There is always, so Holmes believes, something to be done.

Having weighed the evidence, he reaches a firm conclusion. There is an echo here of his namesake, Sherlock. The villa in Tottenham becomes a version of the rooms of the consulting detective in Baker Street. There are constant interruptions of domestic quietude: beggars at the door, confidence men with impossible yarns, broken women. The sturdy Thomas Holmes, more Dr Watson than neurasthenic, cocaine-injecting detective, transcribes the stumbling biographies of human flotsam who float outside official history, the underclass of imperialism. Sad ghosts of those golden summers before the First War changed everything.

London's Underworld carries the dirt and misery of an earlier city: memory traces of Dickens, Gissing, of Jack London's *The People of the Abyss*. But the abyss mapped by Holmes is more than a metaphor. Step out of line, suffer an industrial accident, a whim of fate, and you are gone: without status, dehumanised. Beyond the doubtful sanctuary of cheap rooms and cheaper furniture are the streets, doorways, parks.

You fail and it is absolute. Holmes, prison reformer and secretary of the Howard Association, talks to the incarcerated, offers help to those he deems capable of helping themselves.

This was not the city of railways, electricity, orbital motorways imagined by Ford Madox Ford in *The Soul of London* (1905). Thomas Holmes, born in 1846 (when Dickens was labouring over *Dombey and Son* in Switzerland), outlived Henry James by two years. But his prose is untainted by the ambiguities and self-doubts of Modernism. Freudian psychodramas, Jungian archetypes, the fractured perspectives of Vorticism, do not disturb a philosophy that is grounded in the particulars of locality. Holmes sees it as his business to challenge H.G. Wells, the Wells of *The Time Machine* (1895). 'Are we to have two distinct races! those above and those below? Is Wells' prophecy to come true; will one race become uncanny, loathsome abortions with clammy touch and eyes that cannot face the light?'

The pilgrimage into *London's Underworld* refutes Wellsian determinism: the city is stratified and divided, zones of light and clean air, zones of mephitic darkness, but the divisions can be healed. Holmes tells a plain, unembroidered tale, a report on which we are obliged to act. He cites: Ellen Langes, 59, a blouse-maker of Graham Road, Dalston, who starves to death. She is unable to get work and has sold all her household effects. The authorities show little interest in her case. She dies within sight of the German Hospital where Joseph Conrad was brought after his Congo collapse and where he meditated *The Heart of Darkness*. Not appreciating, perhaps, that it was here all along, within a few yards of his bed. The harsh consequences of shifts in market economics.

Rescued legends from the underworld are most often virtuoso displays of local colour, heroic tourism. The narrator descends from the civilised strata of society for a season and then returns with lurid episodes, sentimental cameos that are intended to shock. Jack London began his Whitechapel voyage, in the summer of 1902, by attending the offices of Thomas Cook. 'I went down into the under-world of

London with an attitude of mind which I may best liken to that of an explorer.' He took his camera, he dressed in borrowed rags. He played a part. George Orwell (name changed, biography suppressed) followed the same path to the kitchens, skips and doss houses. He was fascinated and repelled by an exoticism of otherness. 'The room stank like a ferret's cage,' he wrote. 'You did not notice it when you got up, but if you went out and came back, the smell hit you in the face with a smack.'

There is no role-playing for Holmes. He makes himself known to his prey. He carries loose change. He describes what he sees. And describes it to a purpose: fresh ideas, change, action. Slums must be pulled down. Children freed from prisons. Charity wards will be properly managed. 'Some day when we are wise – but wisdom comes so slowly – these things will not be left to private enterprise, for municipalities will provide and own them at no loss to ratepayers either.'

When Holmes displays the gifts of a novelist, he is most engaging: he confesses his gullibility and promotes a kind of free-spirited vagrancy he knows must be lost. He can, at times, sound like a social engineer, a eugenicist. 'I do not recommend a lethal chamber, but I do strongly advise permanent detention and segregation for those low types of unfortunate humanity.' But he speaks from what he has seen and never allows dogma to betray his quirky humanity.

This man with a passport to the lower depths meets Angus, an apparently blind seaman, who wanders the suburbs, 'looking for Bridlington on the road to Southgate.' Holmes knows he is being tricked, but he can't resist the lovely pitch. 'Its very audacity ensures success.' He stands at his Tottenham doorway, in dressing-gown and slippers, and offers charity to this ancient mariner with a story. And for that reason, for the spirit with which he pits himself against mock-piety and prejudice, we can forgive him anything. Even his reluctant assertion that all such wanderers should be removed from the public highway. We must, he concludes, establish 'special colonies for vagrants.' Holding camps, asylums. 'Every vagrant who could not give proof that he had some definite object in tramping must be committed to these colonies and detained, till such time as definite occupation or home can be found for him.'

Such are the complexities, the problems for anyone proposing a solution to injustice, to the sickness and poverty Holmes discovered in his underworld. The villains and the wanderers or London are always present, moving at the edge of things, the limits of visibility. Men of large sympathy, drawn as much to write as to act, are their only witnesses. Their celebrants.

Jack Kerouac

LONESOME TRAVELLER (1960):
KEROUAC'S LONDON DÉRIVE

'He summed up his position in a stern pronouncement,' Bruce Chatwin said of Werner Herzog. 'Walking is virtue, tourism is deadly sin.' Herzog, bad shoes, the clothes he stood up in, tramped from Munich to Paris, in a winter pilgrimage to rescue the critic Lotte Eisner from a terminal diagnosis. 'She will not die, I will not permit it.'

Jack Kerouac, in *The Dharma Bums, Desolation Angels* and elsewhere, was never far from his hiking boots: unlaced, blistered leather with flapping tongue. Rucksack, sleeping bag, notebook. An elective sadhu, Buddhist-Catholic, trapped between the real world and the mythology he contrived to appease it. Friends and acquaintances were assigned their roles in the soap-opera seizure of a new *Pilgrim's Progress* unravelling across the fabulous spread of the post-war American landscape. Hydrogen jukeboxes. Oasis gas stations out of Robert Mitchum *film noir*. Voodoo priests kneeling in supplication beside the restless Mississippi. Kerouac road-tested brand names, retro-styles and hair attitudes of the distant future. Unlike Burroughs, he didn't live long enough to advertise Nike trainers.

Life, which is another word for work, truth-breath, was not great in 1957. Kerouac's abortive European tour, that spring, proved to be his last season as a writer who existed inside the protective and self-affirming nest of unpublished fiction: before the devastating flash-exposure of fame. With that much-delayed arrival of *On the Road*. Here was success, hungry and insatiable, on a scale unprecedented until you go back to Scott Fitzgerald, another drinker destroyed by his status as the voice of a generation. Prophesies that can be confirmed only by the public death, in shame and obscurity, of the nominated author. Stupid arguments in Florida bars for Jack, redneck roleplay: *Miami Vice* in a lumberjack shirt, untucked over the impressive contours of a beer gut. And, in Fitzgerald's case, Hollywood hackdom. Faustian contracts celebrated in baths of Tokay wine and intravenous whisky. Editors, publicists, agents pimping top-dollar gigs with mind-sucking magazines. Lawyers demanding affidavits for portraits contrived in the bitter validation of poetry.

'World travel isn't as good as it seems,' confessed Jack. Neurotic migration – car loaded with mother's furniture, Greyhound bus, Yugoslav steamer reeling across the Atlantic – is a symptom and not a solution. Tangier, after all, is what it ought to be, a North African port, a sink for exiles and hustlers. The Paris Kerouac endured was straight from the brochure, a weary fondness for cultural values written up in vanished books. *Lonesome Traveller*, a collection of occasional pieces, disposable or inspired drudgery, was a wounding experience. Fat cheques for thin words.

But the knowledge that one day, in April 1957, Kerouac walked through London, from Victoria Station (where the boat train from Newhaven arrived) to St Paul's Cathedral, haunted me. This ancient, endlessly overlaid river settlement is mapped by walkers and the stories they tell, myths shaped from fallible memory. As Kerouac took the tourist trail to the east, so the ghost of Samuel Pepys (who went to school beside St Paul's) moved west, down mud-and-shit-splattered Fleet Street to Westminster. Without comment, Kerouac hauled his pilgrim's pack past the building where William Blake died, in

Fountain Court on the Strand. And past the Eleanor Cross outside Charing Cross Station, which many take as a marker for the centre of the city. Past the house where Pepys grew up. Past the round Temple Church with its slumbering crusaders. And in parallel, all the way, with the Thames, which Kerouac neither notices nor acknowledges.

To the north of his route is the room where Thomas De Quincey, the definitive walking writer of the urban labyrinth, sweated over *Confessions of an English Opium Eater*. In becoming, like William Burroughs, addiction itself, hungry for hunger, cells screaming, De Quincey lifts hackwork, words as coins, to visionary levels. He self-plagiarises, gossips about friends, digresses and strides forward with the velocity of Kerouac's prime model, Louis-Ferdinand Céline. Jack is never more than a respectful tourist in London, killing time before returning home, to face the consequences of fame. The exiled Céline, shrapnel in skull, spitting out ellipses like hot rivets, carves a series of furious trajectories across the city. There is nothing to touch those novels, *Guignol's Band* and *London Bridge*. Our capital has never quite lived up to them.

Well aware, on the morning of September 1, 2009, that I was a ghost among ghosts, I set out to follow in Kerouac's London footprints. The problem being that I knew too much. Almost every yard of this route was part of the narrative of forty years in one city. Freshly arrived from Dublin in 1966, I accompanied a friend called Chris to the offices of the publisher André Deutsch in Great Russell Street. Chris, on my recommendation, was delivering his first novel, hundreds of typed pages in a blue shirtbox. Who better than the firm responsible for English editions of Kerouac? Beckett and Kafka were the big influences for Chris. We argued over my unshakeable enthusiasm for free-flowing spontaneous prose. Burroughs was fine, Chris reckoned, since he was published in olive-green wrappers by the Olympia Press in Paris. Located in Tangier, Mr Burroughs sent a lovely three-column text to Dublin. No more was heard of Chris's novel and he never wrote another.

Drawn east by the gravity of monuments, the choir who would perform *St Matthew's Passion* in St Paul's on Good Friday, Kerouac was a hiking tourist, a category foreign to Herzog. He noticed Buckingham Palace, Trafalgar Square, Dr Johnson's Fleet Street and the King Lud pub at the foot of Ludgate Hill. He was innocent of the plaque for a different breed of mythologist, Edgar Wallace, and innocent too of the window where peasant-poet John Clare stared in mesmerised fascination at the passing crowds. Like Kerouac, Clare was a toy of fame, driven mad by the demands of sudden and random celebrity. Then cast aside: the long silence of the Northampton asylum.

Using Kerouac as a guide, navigating by this limited map, I saw how present London folds out from tourist clusters, through the surveillance state, into sponsored public art. Horse-straw in the gutter beside the bomb-deflecting obstacles of Buckingham Palace. Heraldic crockery on display, a half-price sale, in the Royal Mews. Ceremonial cavalry clattering down the Mall. Armed police under Admiralty Arch. A man dressed as the Pink Panther busking on Antony Gormley's plinth in Trafalgar Square. The Eleanor Cross wrapped like a Christo.

The pub where Kerouac enjoyed his stout and Welsh Rarebit is now a fast-food joint called LEON, but Lud's head is still up on the wall as a decorative feature. If Jack had paused at St Dunstan-in-the-West, he could have seen old Lud himself, a blackened symbol of the origin of the city, hidden away in an alcove. This was all he ever wanted, the heart of the quest. Interrogated by John Wingate, a TV talk-show guest, Jack spelled it out: 'I'm waiting for God to show his face.'

Arthur Machen

OUR UNKNOWN EVERYWHERE

I'm here in Housmans Bookshop, drawing breath against the conflicted microclimate of the never-satisfied development vortex around King's Cross Station, because this is a special place; an oasis that allows urban wanderers to step aside from the dust and swirl of the street – and, at the same time, to enter a cave that is, through its curation of lost texts, its gathering of alert and voluble citizens, an extension of that street. I mean that the shop is radical, dissenting, and well supplied with primers for subversion. It stands witness to an old and threatened tradition: the provision of reading matter for rail journeys by way of shelves of reforgotten writers, pamphlets left behind with no expectation of a sale. The choice of a book should involve a degree of occult speculation. You are looking for whatever it is that you don't know you need. You solicit the unexpected, something convenient to carry on a risky expedition to a place you have never visited. Didn't Arthur Machen say it for us? 'All the wonders lie within a stone's throw of King's Cross Station.' The miraculous mundane. The loose paving stone that acts as a trapdoor to the underworld. The terminus that might be terminal.

I never break a walk, by calling here for a quick scan of the stock, and go away empty handed. This is a London tactic refined by Arthur Machen, our man of the west: the ability to drift, to sleepwalk in other people's sleep. To recognise holy hills behind a sprawl of suburbs. To register the precise degree of luminescence in bones under those hills. Machen turned restlessness and the metropolitan ennui of a fading imperial capital to account: hours, stolen from some dreary money-earning task, spent wandering and wondering through the labyrinth – or beyond it, when there was no task and few coins to jingle in the pocket. Time to explore, accumulate impressions, throw off conditioned reflexes. To slump, alone or with a companion in idleness, in a previously unvisited hostelry that must never be found again. 'And in spite of the routine of the City, the counting of coupons, and all the mechanical drudgery that had lasted for ten years,' Machen wrote in 'A Fragment of Life', 'there still remained about him the curious hint of wild grace, as if he had been born a creature of the antique wood, and had seen the fountain rising from the green moss and grey rocks.'

'There is a tavern in the north-western parts of London which is so remote from the tracks of men and so securely hidden that few people ever suspect its existence.' That tavern is located in the opening paragraph, the hook, of *The London Adventure*. Books, moving both ways in time, prospecting the past while acting as a goad to the future, are a necessary cartography for any life trapped within the gravity-field of an ever-expanding city. Machen understood the equation perfectly. He had experienced most of the aspects of the trade: as author, translator, editor, promoter, journalist, performer, dealer, collector. And then, at the end of it all, as *presence*. One of those mysterious beings that become a subject for academic research and amateur detection. Some writers – and Machen is certainly of their company – enter a sort of Swedenborgian twilight, in which they are eternally present, neither alive nor dead, a shadowy immanence on a favoured street. They are always being republished, reinvented, resurrected in gaudy paperbacks and limited editions. Before winking and disappearing once more into bibliographic rumour. They are so obliging, these spectres, like Stevenson and De Quincey and Conan Doyle; they fade into their own fictions, to emerge as entities from a parallel universe. They belong to the eternal *now* – like beings trapped in a perpetual *Coronation Street*, in which newspapers crumble to dust while the actors never acquire another wrinkle.

Machen is a benign actor from a more literary past, the unreachable regions of a city of memory reconstructed from lost libraries. The Xanadu of quotations. He is no longer a voter, a ratepaying statistic. He is an Arthur Machen character in a never-completed dialogue between Clerkenwell and Caerleon, Llanthony Priory and Limehouse: possession and renunciation. He can be adapted to fit the fashion of the moment.

Merlin Coverley sees him as moving alongside us through the crowd – perhaps tipping his hat for a moment at the back of this bookshop – 'within the tradition of writer as walker.' But there are also those penitential rooms, out in the dreaming suburbs, or sooty-windowed in Bloomsbury, where Machen is a prisoner of words, trapped at his desk, burrowing away at the latest commission. Sometimes he stands and watches the flow. And sometimes a contemporary London wanderer, as he makes his way home down Gray's Inn Road, imagines that short, stocky outline; a teasing shape projected by firelight onto dirty blinds. Machen is a writer who is capable of noticing us, anticipating our future trajectories, years before we have been born. That's what a London presence is: a writer who becomes writing.

There has been a fissure in the nature of things this week, so it's probably a good time to think again about Machen. The icy chills have relented, but all around me friends are involved in strange accidents. Andrew Kötting, the gallivanting film-maker with whom I've collaborated, most recently on a swan-pedalo voyage from Hastings to Hackney, came off his motorbike on the Old Kent Road; a serious shunt, skidding across tarmac, bike toppling onto him, severing an artery in the leg, fracturing an elbow.

I think of my Kötting escapades as having a Machenesque quality:

walks through landscapes with a borderland feel and mysterious characters emerging from the mist to launch unprompted into tall tales.

Kötting is recovering now, he was saved by the fact that he was in a part of London where there was so much aggravation, the police were all over. He was treated by an efficient Polish officer and rushed to hospital. The same hospital, coincidentally, that we had passed, a few weeks before, when I persuaded Andrew to undergo a one-day circumambulation around London's Overground Railway. Such walks, as Machen understood better than anybody, provoke an overlapping series of autobiographical anecdotes, past-life confessions. The walkers draw breath by taking turns to spin a yarn. Memories emerge from the territory through which we hike. Talk about a hospital and you'll be back in it very soon. Pubs and cafés are not just repositories for boasts and gossip, but also chambers in which the movement of the walk, the sounds and smells and impressions, can unravel and take new forms.

In the early Sixties when I was a film student in Brixton, and later as a used-book dealer in Islington, Machen was coming at me from so many directions. I traded enthusiasms with Brian Catling, when we worked in the ullage cellar at Truman's Brewery in Brick Lane. I found William Hope Hodgson's *The House on the Borderland* on a market stall in Kingsland Waste. I also came across a 1923 reprint of Machen's *The House of Souls* with striking, cloth-covered pictorial boards. In this case the book had been used at some point for darts practice, the sharp points had penetrated as far as the title page. Perhaps somebody used darts as a form of divination? Flipping the pages I came on: 'It was soon after I had left this town behind me that I found the Strange Road.' Which I took as permission for launching a walk around the acoustic footprints of London's orbital motorway, the M25. Meanwhile, Catling accumulated a raft of H.P. Lovecraft paperbacks, Algernon Blackwood in hardback, and a fine edition of Edgar Allan Poe's *The Raven* with illustrations by Arthur Rackham.

In more recent times, Brian has established a considerable reputation as performance artist, sculptor, poet and novelist. He operates as head of sculpture at the Ruskin School of Drawing and Fine Art in Oxford. I visited Oxford. I'd agreed to look at the work of three promising and very different artists. The last of the three, when I was already reeling from the challenge of two intense hours of discussion, with inadequate attempts on my part to forge a useful response to presentations that were locked in to their own devices and strategies, was a young woman who did things with flies. Or so it struck me. Webs across windows. Minute beings testing the limits of vision. 'Boschian battles between insects and tiny winged skeletal humanoids.' The thing that needed to be said was: absolutely nothing. This world in miniature required no superfluous commentary. Any word on my part would be too large and lumbering for the context. That was the charm of the elegant and filmy-tough traps that had insinuated their way into the alcoves of the Oxford building and out into various trees and parks and greens.

'I'd like to show you some books,' the young woman said. So I replied, 'Great, I like seeing books.' I took them as they were passed to me and opened them with care, dealer-fashion, with no risk of breaking the spines or leaving dirty thumbprints. Arthur Machen! First editions with presentation inscriptions. The artist's name was Tessa Farmer, the great-granddaughter of Machen. Now it made sense. The reason why Catling had invited me to engage with this particular maker. And, beyond that, the startling and original nature of Tessa's art. This technically skilled conjuring of haunted scenarios like grids contrived to catch unseen beings. It was perfect. Tessa is now a starry figure, collected by the Saatchi Gallery and acquired by the Ashmolean Museum. It was only when a member of The Friends of Arthur Machen drew her attention to the areas of sympathy between her own work and that of her great-grandfather that she began to read his books. The episode climaxed an extraordinary morning for me. The excitement of having these books with Machen's marks and signatures in my hands – and then learning that one of his direct descendants was still making magical borderland art!

*

But the crucial one, and the book I want to concentrate on even though it's not one of Machen's great pieces, is *The London Adventure or The Art of Wandering* – which could also be called *The Art of Digression*: a technique I've borrowed, and which, as you'll notice, I'm still employing. It's about negative capability, operating within our doubts, against the grain of the times. It's about how to get lost creatively, how to navigate through a web of coincidences and confusions, and how to live and thrive in a plural city where all of these things happen at once. I'd like to call up the 1970s, the period evoked by some of the publications you see at the desk in Housmans. We've come full circle; some young, active, smart kids are beginning to produce books, right outside the mainstream; books that look like those crafted in the Sixties and Seventies; all shapes and sizes, kitchen-table collated and stapled, smudgy wafers of things that are so spontaneous and immediate and of the moment. The product now is much slicker, referencing what went before but exploiting the enhanced technology of the digital age. The spirit of the publications I was doing through Albion Village Press in the 1970s is respectfully invoked. I like that. I like the fact that there are young poets around who are drawing on Barry MacSweeney and Bill Griffiths. And new readers of the London labyrinth going back to Machen: writers and artists and performers as smart, and as diverse, as Alan Moore and Stewart Lee. And in that sense the story isn't over. It remains open-ended: Moore could very easily co-opt Machen into his *The League of Extraordinary Gentlemen*. Michael Moorcock, within the spiral paths of his multiverse, could send his own characters, Jerry Cornelius or Sir Seaton Begg, back into a tale already composed by Machen. Nothing is final. While there are still engaged readers to be found, the writing stays open. 'The Friends of Arthur Machen' sounds like code for a Masonic cabal described by G.K. Chesterton or an unwritten Sherlock Holmes story rescued from a pulped copy of *Beeton's Christmas Annual*.

To earn the wages to publish these fugitive books, I would take any jobs that were going – with the notion, always, of exploring a new part of East London, gaining access to some secret world. Gardening in Limehouse, labouring in Truman's Brewery, cigar-packing in Clerkenwell. On your bike. Keep moving. A few weeks, a few months: money for another Albion Village Press production. I landed one of the best of these jobs on Hackney Marshes. Two hundred football pitches. Start on Monday morning. I painted the white lines, a week of the purest meditation under wide skies in the now dispersed glory of the Lower Lea Valley. Constable cloud forms and weather systems. The best kind of durational cinema. The Lower Lea Valley is my golden terrain, its potency enhanced by the recent enclosures, dust storms, pollution of waterways, hundreds of dead fish. Hackney Marshes was my equivalent for Machen's shimmering memories of the Welsh borders. His woods and hills. The Marshes were commonplace, marked out by post-industrial relics, concrete wartime pillboxes, pylon forests, knotweed jungles, but they had some element of the mystery Machen describes with such lyrical force. 'And I went on, and at last I found a certain wood, which is too secret to be described, and nobody knows of the passage into it, which I found out in a very curious manner...' Walking through the lammas lands of the Lower Lea Valley sustained that potentiality: a green path, a hollow way, a thorn tunnel giving entrance to another reality, to a grove of shadows and stillness, where the muffled crump of traffic becomes a natural sound like running water.

So I was painting these white lines, it was like being responsible for the Nazca lines in the Atacama Desert. At the end of the week fools would rush in with their footballs and kick my artwork to pieces, and I would start my labour of repair once again the next morning.

Anyway, I got home to Hackney one night, and there weren't really many cars on the street in those days, but outside the house was a royal-blue Rolls Royce Corniche. I didn't know whether my wife had won the pools while I'd been out or if the property had been repossessed, and we'd been expelled, and plutocratic incomers had taken over. It got worse. There was a man who'd bluffed his way through the door with some unlikely tale about how he needed to talk to me, urgently, about a project to reignite the spiritual energies of London. He was sitting comfortably in my room, going through the books, along with his sidekick, a bearded, pipe-sucking, sweating figure in a heavy duffle coat.

The younger man, the one in the leather jacket, with the lizard-flicking eyes and coiled energies, leapt to his feet and challenged me with a single question. 'Do you like John Cowper Powys?' I jumped back. I actually had a few Powys titles within reach, so this was good, he was convinced. 'Right, come down to Chelsea tomorrow. To the offices in King's Road. You're on the payroll. Fifty notes a week.' He was a rag-trade millionaire who'd suddenly had 'the vision' – which was basically John Cowper Powys. Powys would be the titular spirit for a spanking new flagship shop on Regent Street. With Japanese fishpond, Powys bust, portraits. The man's name was Jeff Kwintner, his attendant poet and cultural adviser was Hugo Manning.

Slipstreaming Powys would be Henry Miller, Kenneth Patchen, Alfred Perlés – and Arthur Machen. Jeff said: 'One of the first things I want you to do is to go round to your printers on Balls Pond Road, we're going to reissue this little book called *The London Adventure.*' In that way, my own Albion Village Press was immediately followed by Kwintner's Village Press. The book, if I remember it, emerged with a silvery cover, a paperback. I hadn't read it, now it became a provocation, an excuse to start walking the northwest suburbs, the slumberland territories where Jeff lived. Radlett. And the road out. All the way to St Albans. Over motorways, through golf courses. And immaculate unpeopled villages.

I'd got the Machen book published by this madman who'd put me on the payroll, cash-money every Thursday – and then he hands me the keys to a red Ferrari and a new tape recorder, and he tells me to go to Blaenau Ffestiniog and find Phyllis Playter, the mistress of Cowper Powys and to do an interview with her. I disappear into the Welsh mountains for weeks, and come back, like a broken private detective, and he said, 'No no no, forget that. You don't understand.' Finger to lips. Another plastic beaker of champagne. Another phone call. 'Don't say it. What do you want, your name in lights? We need *big* photographs of Avebury and Sudbury Hill and Stonehenge and something on the Marx Brothers and then W.C. Fields. *Go go go*. We're off to the Sherlock Holmes pub. Then we're doing Machen and London walks. Start at Gray's Inn Road. What do you think about Castaneda? The Albigensians? Allen Ginsberg? Steiner? Jung's *Alchemical Studies*? Borges? Fred Astaire?' This was the brief flare of a London of conspiracies and manic energies when everything was possible, everybody would come onboard: Colin Wilson, Angus Wilson, Wilson Knight, all the Wilsons. And it circled around the theory and practice of *The London Adventure*. Great times hurtling towards the big black hole. Village Press dead stock heaped in bundles on Farringdon Road. All the participants in rehab or expelled to New York with suitcases of unsold paperbacks.

That was beginning and I never forgot the first sentence of Kwintner's Machen book about that tavern hidden among the northwestern parts of London. I can't quote it exactly because my memory's gone. I do recall that Machen moves on very rapidly. He talks about 'the streets of which I meant to write: unknown, unvisited squares in Islington, dreary byways in Holloway, places traversed by railway arches and viaducts in the regions of Camden Town.'

'Everything was shapeless,' he continues, 'unmeaning, dreary, dismal beyond words; it was as if one were journeying past the back wall of the everlasting backyard.' I was completely sold on that. I don't think I got much further, that's it, the recognition that London has a meaning 'beyond words' and that it is our task to find words to express it. Identify the right pub, in the right corner of an obscure suburb, and the paragraphs dictate themselves. Walker as writer as medium. The act of tramping will call up *presences*, earlier authors with uncompleted projects, loose sheets to be collated into new combinations. Figures like Robert Louis Stevenson, Coleridge, De Quincey. And Machen.

London is a labyrinth, it's a construct, and all the writers who get sucked into dealing with this thing, the blind alleys, dead-ends, windowless courtyards, eventually encounter a *figure*, a shape emerging from the hallucinatory geometric patterns. You feel the gravity, the insistent pull of the Northwest Passage, the whisperings of hidden rivers. The Northwest Passage becomes a metaphor for the quest, based on actual voyages by the early venturers, Sir Hugh Willoughby, Martin Frobisher, John Franklin. You infiltrate zones of covert narrative, the undescribed, the unwritten, the unrecorded. The parts of Hackney and Stoke Newington that Machen touches on in his influential tale, 'N'. The story works so well because it echoes Edgar Allen Poe's 'William Wilson' as well as anticipating works from the period of the psychogeographers. You move through unfamiliar streets in a way that you can only do once. This is not an uncommon London experience.

An important part of my engagement with Machen took place just up the hill from here in Islington. I had a secondhand bookstall in a recently opened book market in Camden Passage. It changed my life, this was the real education. Muddling through an orthodox education, that established form of cultural processing, you are indoctrinated into a bibliography of the canonical texts you are required to read and remember, in order to equip yourself for a career as scholar, school-teacher, copywriter, journalist. I'd sampled the modernists. I read what you were supposed to read, and I'd also snacked on a lot of popular stuff that came my way by accident – but I had not experienced the full anti-pantheon, the outsiders: M.P. Shiel, William Irish, Francis Stuart, Jim Thompson, William Hope Hodgson.

My involvement with Machen was shallow. I had not, at that point, received the hour-long tutorials of the fanatics who would visit my stall and assume that I shared their own passion for a single author. The trade in books initiates a dialogue with what people are actually reading and not what they say they are reading, or are supposed to be reading.

I hadn't discovered Roland Camberton, who published only two books, lively novels of the streets of Bloomsbury and Hackney. I hadn't even started on Alexander Baron. This was my true initiation into the literature of the city: standing for eight or nine hours at a bookstall, every Thursday and Friday, and letting the punters come at you, searching for impossible titles, improbable authors – or talking, wildly, feverishly, in autistic detail, about their *personal* delusions. The writers with whom, after years of reading and rereading, they now claimed a special, near sexual, relationship.

This is a subtle genetic exchange of shared secrets, newly discovered facts, speculative gossip. It's interesting to see that so many of those authors who were recommended to me are now back in print, the writers I call 'the reforgotten'. Someone finds them, puts them out again. I've noticed Alexander Baron's *The Lowlife* come back two or three times; sometimes it almost sticks, sometimes it doesn't, it just disappears. There were certain books that had that quality; certain authors required a fellowship of disciples questing for out-of-print rarities. Machen was perfect material for this treatment: he touched on the deep psychic estrangements of metropolitan life. Horror, war, the occult and the fascinating decadence of the Nineties.

There was a dealer called Martin Stone, one of the best, an authentic scholar as well as a much-admired rock musician. He was a champion of M.P. Shiel – and, through Shiel, Machen. He talked a lot about Machen. He mentioned the retirement to Amersham. I felt that Martin had visited him there, which was of course impossible. Machen died when Stone was less than a year old. But I'm sure Martin sniffed around the traces to see if anything could be found. And anyway, with dealers whose detective skills are supernatural, time is an elastic medium. Such men pop up, in various disguises, across the centuries. They inform the essence of place.

One of my own finds in the territory around Amersham was that pamphlet you probably know called *Writers Take Sides on the Spanish Civil War*. Most of the writers were strongly in favour of the Republic.

I remember Samuel Beckett just said 'Up the Republic!' But there were several exceptions coming out firmly in support of Franco: one as you might expect was Evelyn Waugh, Roy Campbell was another. And then there was Arthur Machen. I can't remember now if it was more of a surprise to find Machen being asked for his opinion at that late stage in his career, or to learn what that opinion was. His position was based on his Catholicism: support for religion, that sense of something hieratic and unchanging offended by the nature of revolution. This minor discovery made me look again at Machen – and at how he stood in the world of realpolitik and paid journalism. These are more complex matters than I had previously appreciated and he's a more complex figure.

Jon Savage, a good cultural critic, and an astute and compulsive collector, picked up some nice Machen items over the years. We would chat on the phone sometimes when he ordered books from my catalogues. 'I used to be obsessed by Machen,' he said, 'but there's something psychically damaging here; I've got to get rid of these things, I can't keep them any more.' That struck home too, and I found an identifiable quality of sadistic repression in certain of the tales. Private surgery as a disturbing ritual. Unstable metaphors worrying around the schizophrenia of the London labyrinth and the hills of memory: a tense dialogue resolved through the infinite boredom of the western suburbs.

I think, in the end, we all identify with particular territories, or recognise certain territories as having narrative potential, half-cooked stories waiting to be found. Some places have a greater somatic density, because of concentrated human activity. Areas where there's been so much hard labour; so much pain and fear and exhaustion. You can still pick up on the electro-magnetic waves of decommissioned madhouses, hospitals and prisons. If you are out on the ragged fringes of London, it's much harder to quantify. The human traces are often obscured by predatory development. I feel, quite strongly, the way the current moves between the inner city of business and the liminal zones around and beyond the M25, the orbital motorway.

There's a kind of London writing crafted by people like Derek Raymond, in the tradition originated by Julian Maclaren-Ross: you go into Soho, into the pub at opening time, and you absorb, without lifting your elbow from the bar, all the chat, the drama, the comedy and the craziness of the city. You perch and sway until closing time. You take the last train, the Tube, to the suburbs. You get it all down, hot. You write through the night, processing this material into a formal structure. Then you go back the next day and do it all again. Raymond often spoke about the 'general contract': mortality. You're here, at the bar, among friends. Then you're dead. But the general contract also applies to the writer. History is the medium in which you swim. You exploit it. It chews you up. You die.

So, as a defensive mechanism, you move around the labyrinth; you retreat to some quiet suburban cave and process the noise, the mess. I couldn't do that, but there have been many, many London writers who manage it very successfully. They're ventriloquising the city and its whispers, the secrets and conspiracies and confessions of people who are never going to write. We find our own techniques. This is all I'm trying to say: keep history alive, document whatever is within your reach, be suspicious of dogma. And anyone who tells you that he (or she) has the answer.

Michael Moorcock

MOTHER LONDON (1988)

James Joyce claimed that the sea-town of Dublin, once destroyed, could rise again out of the pages of *Ulysses*. Michael Moorcock, with transcendent modesty, brings to life the ravished and abused confederation of villages that make up his *Mother London* from the unregarded stock of some prelapsarian Portobello junk-pit.

He decorates its groves and dales with glittering toys and tricks, *Magnets* and *Gems*, strands of detonated old boys' fiction, fire-damaged ephemera. He honours the underground rivers, forgotten music halls, parks, pubs and mythic fathers. This is a book that has been assembling itself for years, while Moorcock readied himself to discover it. It is the achievement of a master craftsman at the height of his powers: made possible by the length and diversity of his career, the training in compression, serial-composition, jump-cut and sheer elbows-on-the-table, hook-'em-hard narrative drive.

Mother London is an unhurried epic that calmly, and at conversational pitch, manipulates the stream of time between the twinned traumas of Blitz and Blight; from the stern alchemy of fire-storms to the corrupt transformation of the city as a fatally tainted heritage riverscape. The conscience of ruin invades our galloping entropy with mantic and urgent voices-in-the-head: 'must stop this going back to I was happy why can't I accept the present.' What was once heroic and human is now savage and self-serving. The threat is ourselves, our loss of nerve. These pilgrims are disenfranchised and crazy like foxes.

It is, of course, a millennial version of where-did-we-go-wrong, but also, and primarily, it celebrates the journey, relishing the pricks of the flesh, the pains and joys of those who are condemned to live up to their own obsessions. They will not blaspheme against the self-mutilating impulses that are their only guide. So this tale of many voices is built up from the overlapping biographies of a group of perpetual outpatients who wander the limits of the city like exiles from Blake's *Jerusalem*, tossed from Jack Straw's Castle to Bedlam, from Kensal Rise to Bethnal Green, lighting up 'every Minute Particular of Albion degraded.'

They are the lesser gods of Moorcock's Mahabharata, coupling, betraying, discovering and, endlessly, talking. They are richly and sensuously named: Joseph Kiss, Mary Gasalee, David Mummer – who seems, in part, an avatar of the author, 'calling himself an urban anthropologist... lives by writing memorials to legendary London.' They feed on seizures that occurred during the fire-raids. They have alternately raged and sleepwalked through the dying fall of the years that followed.

Mary Gasalee walked, unharmed, from the inferno of her bombed home, with her infant daughter in her arms, only to pass through the welfare state in cyclic dreams of Gamages department store and a visionary Holborn Viaduct, guided and comforted by the presence of familiar afternoon stars, Katharine Hepburn, Janet Gaynor and Merle Oberon, whose name is as rich and strange as her own. Now the city of the apocalypse is invaded by angelic and demonic entities that touch and smile. Mary does not age, becoming a sister to her daughter – and, when she wakes, the lover of both Kiss and the virgin Mummery.

The sympathetic strength of the women, and the delirious wanderings of the men, give the book a warmth that cannot disguise the knowledge that the city, *Mother London* herself, is doomed. The characters are somehow posthumous, glad ghosts. They have a neurotic sensitivity to the colours, tastes and smells of their own small patch of earth. Their abilities as mediums for the voices of the unborn and the dead only bring them pain. They are breakfasting in the flight path of an already-launched V2 rocket. All history is compressed into the breath of a single moment of time.

Beyond them, at the fringe, are the Travellers, the immigrants, the criminals whose collective pasts are now denied and invalidated. Beneath them is a network of abandoned railway tunnels and dead rivers in which survive an underclass of mute tribesmen; a metaphor perhaps for the genre fiction that Moorcock once practised with such distinction, before making his assault on mainstream literature.

This man has the energy of a Golden Age author, whose belief in the validity of fiction as an agent of transformation is breathtaking in its optimism. If any of the debased literary prizes want to make a claim on credibility they had better put *Mother London* at the head of the list for 1988.

KING OF THE CITY (2000)

Around the time of the London mayoral election, that stupendous non-event in the calendar of civic discourse, posters appeared out of nowhere with the head of a man who wasn't quite Frank Dobson. There was nothing peevish or pop-eyed about this citizen. The shirt was open-necked. The tilted look was watchful, eyes narrowed against bright light: a non-combatant shocked to find himself exposed on the hustings. No Londoner, according to the spin-doctors, is ever going to vote for a beard. The candidate, a Father Christmas in civvies, knows that better than anyone, knows he's on a loser, but it hasn't dowsed his fire. Actually, this fly-pitched outlaw, spotted on the side of a telephone junction box outside Toynbee Hall, on Commercial Street in Whitechapel, had been got up to look like a Wanted poster. Dead or alive. 'Vote Michael Moorcock,' it said. 'King of the City.'

King of the City, a hefty London novel, character-packed, busy with competing narratives (confessing, denouncing, celebrating, plea-bargaining for its own sanity), was being punted by its publicists as 'the long-awaited sequel to a Whitbread Prize shortlisted book *Mother London*.' Clearly, it is nothing of the sort. Prequel, coda, kissing cousin? Arguably. *Mother London* required no sequel. It could have used some of the fortuitous timing that allows a book to mop up well-deserved honours and achieve a word-of-mouth readership that keeps it running for years. Unfortunately, *Mother London* was swamped by the extra-literary controversies surrounding *The Satanic Verses*. One strand in Salman Rushdie's novel, necessarily under-discussed, was based around Brick Lane, a Bollywood dérive through the territory where I came across Moorcock's *King of the City* poster. Both authors have moved on. Rushdie, seduced by the high-definition celebrity culture of New York City, new smells, brighter lights, has denounced his old midden for its failure to fire his imagination – but Moorcock, in whatever exile he finds himself, returns obsessively to his dream-source, the city of his birth.

Mother London, a book whose reputation continued to grow as it became harder to find, as paperbacks disappeared and first editions drifted into charity shops, has now been reissued. Its status as one of the novels by which a substantial portion of London memory can be recovered is assured. The book is a great, humane document, written at a time when the old liberties were under threat and therefore more alive than ever. *Mother London* pivoted on the Blitz, on psychic damage, small urban miracles worked by human affection, a woman walking out of the fire with a newborn baby in her arms. The novel's trajectory of hurt runs from Thatcher's denial of the concept of society, the unappeased demons of the free market, to the communality of war and the shaky utopianism of Old Labour's green lungs, swimming-pools and bright new housing projects.

King of the City is a very different beast. 'Believe me, pards,' it opens, 'we're living in an age of myths and miracles.' (Moorcock knows perfectly well, after all those years of TV evangelists and Teflon politicos, how to manage the spin that sends a sentence into reverse, like a backward-travelling bullet. 'Believe me' means: 'Here we go again. I'm fibbing about fibbing'). Many of the miracles and most of the myths have long since been exploited by Moorcock in fables of sword and sorcery, the reality-collages of the Jerry Cornelius saga, the dark shadows of the Pyat quartet. But the salutation at the start of this new epic is unexpected: 'pard'. Moorcock likes to get the story rolling by speaking directly, as writer and performer, to his audience. His 12-part serial for DC Comics, *Michael Moorcock's Multiverse*, irises-in on the author's head, floating over the walls of a pink city. 'I'm Michael Moorcock. People ask where I get my ideas. Some I find here in Marrakesh.' Next seen on a camel, the narrator aligns himself with storytellers who play 'the mythical game of time.' An Occidental Haroun, he wears a broad-brimmed Indiana Jones hat. He's a role player, a trans-dimensional tourist. Hence the language. 'Pard', according to Jonathon Green's *Dictionary of Slang*, has no existence outside the fictionalised Wild West. Moorcock is like one of those local library researchers from the bosky suburbs, from Norbury or Bexley Heath, churning out tumbleweed romances. Except that his stetson is genuine, off-highway dude store, and his *Tales from the Texas Woods* (1997) were published in Austin and composed in Bastrop, in a Greek Revival mansion that once belonged to Joseph Sayers, a former Governor of Texas.

Such are the jump-cuts of a career begun as a teenager when Moorcock hacked out *Tarzan Adventures*, Sexton Blake thrillers and camp-fire yarns of the purple sage. 'At the age of 17, sitting in a dark little room in South London in the late 1950s,' he wrote in the introduction to *Tales from the Texas Woods*, 'I earned a wonderful living writing about an Arizona I'd never visited, about the Apache and the Comanche, about the torments of the Texas weather. I retailed bits of prairie lore to boys who had as much direct experience of Western life as I had.' This same smooth-cheeked Kane of the Surrey hills makes a fleeting guest appearance in *King of the City*. The hero, Denny Dover, a paparazzo (and proud of it) visiting a Holborn publisher, bumps into a 'fat little office boy who wanted me to think he was the editor.' That's Moorcock in the days when he was dragged along to blackshirt meetings by his editor, W. Howard Baker, 'just for the beer'; and before he chucked his typewriter out of the office window and resigned, bunking off to a life of three-day novellas, quick money and lightning debts.

Dissolve and fast-forward: now it's an age of smooth men, of judgments based on appearance. Commentators are quick to read the signs, the measured droop of Lord Bragg's handkerchief, the precise organisation of Tony Blair's latest consensus hair policy, Lord Archer's ironic, pre-penitentiary crop, the way Andrew Motion carries off his loden coat as he swirls between taxi and station platform. Julian Barnes's novels are depilated at source, fat-free. Frisking them for a Moorcockian digression, a set of cellulite-heavy parentheses, would be like checking a tub of margarine for a stray pubic hair. Smoothness, the absence of bumps and flaws and evidence of facial baroque, is everything. Frank Dobson was doomed as a mayoral contender by his cheek-fuzz, the grimy shadow-scurf of committee rooms and late night arguments that left crumbs in the grizzled thatch. Ken Livingstone razor-swiped his upper lip and found a loose-fitting beige suit to announce (for those who know that public language no longer registers) his readiness to appease, to become a mayor substitute, the political equivalent of decaf.

Moorcock resolutely defies makeover, in depth of chin duvet or in density of luxuriant, hirsute prose. The rings, the scarfs, the tattoos: they don't come off. The portraits of the author in successive novels defiantly parade his period recidivism: grey-flecked beard, shades and Lawrence of Arabia head-towel for the Saudi arms dealer look; sun-bleached chest-curls for the stroller in Mediterranean gardens; *Wild Bunch* outrider, Slim Pickens or Chill Wills with badlands barbering. Moorcock has more hats than Winston Churchill. He distrusts expensive eau de Cologne newcomers with their anorexic novellas: no gravitas, no gravy. He despises the nouvelle cuisine portions served up on mid-culture chat shows. Down there, through the blistering Texas summers in the Bastrop bunker, he needs Radio 4 to keep him sane, to keep him in touch with the metropolitan discourse he walked away from. He can't abide the smoothies, the slenderness of their emotions, the tricksy little paragraphs; the lack of liver and lights, refried potatoes, heart-attack breakfasts served up in a cellar beneath Smithfield market. Moorcock's distemper remains, despite the viral assaults of life in a genetically-modified George W. Bush fiefdom (fevers, sweats, steroid-regimens), genially satiric rather than venomous and bile-secreting; he targets the virtual reality spooks of Lit-Lite. The fawn jackets. The suit-bags. The shaved sentences.

English fiction (the creative reading list), as he satirises it in *King of the City*, acquires an energy that it would not otherwise espouse. Here is the unreconstructed 'engine of comedy', Rex Martin ('the famous farting novelist') and his diminutive son, Felix. Here is 'Jillian Burnes', a transsexual romancer. But these knockabout cartoons are absorbed into a chiaroscuro of the forgotten, denizens of the deep recalled and re-remembered. The faces of the moment occupy less space than the invisibles, colleagues of the author, the ungrateful dead who won't leave him alone. 'Send for the resurrection men,' says Denny Dover. 'My nobody friends are dying by the day.' There is, within the volatile structure of *King of the City*, a tyranny of nostalgia, too many bleak afternoons spent in Kensal Green crematorium. 'Nothing,' the narrator announces, 'is more important than talk.' Reading Moorcock's novel is like eavesdropping on a remorseless, unforgiving monologue, an extraordinary séance, a memory stunt summoning all the ghosts of his long career, his busy life. The writer Jack Trevor Story is presented as a moral touchstone, the exemplar of a better period – jazz, film-scripts, novels sold three times over under different titles; the third wife, the fifth bankruptcy. The sidebars have sidebars, addenda foliate in Mandelbrotian chaos; the narrative folds back on itself, excusing and exploiting well-worn anecdotes. Moorcock sketches his version of the late Derek Raymond (a.k.a. Robin Cook) as a Soho revenant: 'Cookie was still alive in those days . . . and telling your stories back to you faster than you could recount them.'

Much of *King of the City* is like that, using the 'twist' to reconstitute chat rehearsed by Moorcock in the oxygen debt of endless interviews, interrogations at Fantasy conventions, comfortable reminiscences over the teacups. The story that Mai Zetterling told of her encounter with Peter Sellers and Kingsley Amis, at the time of the filming of *Only Two Can Play*, moves easily from life to fiction. 'Want to see my Aertexes?' asks the disgraceful Rex Martin, the Amis offprint. What happens is that world fits within world like a series of Russian dolls, the living and the dead, the improbable and the impossible, doubles, doppelgängers, fetches, fabulous parasites who improve on their mundane originals. Moorcock calls the system his 'multiverse': a near-infinite nest of universes, each only marginally different from the next and only widely different when separated by millions of variants, where time is not linear but a field in which all these universes rest, creating the appearance of linearity within their own small sphere; where sometimes groups of universes exist in full knowledge and in full intercourse with the others, where 'rogue' universes can take sideways orbits, crashing through the dimensions and creating all kinds of disruptions in the delicate fabric of space-time.

It reads tougher than it plays. The hook and the base narrative of *King of the City* are pretty straight: the story is being told in a lilac-tinted present, somewhere in the aftermath of the death of 'the People's Princess.' Denny Dover (patriotic surname, English chalk running through it like lettering in Brighton rock), ex-musician, ex-name photographer, current burnout, lucks onto a great scoop: a supposedly dead Murdoch-substitute being pleasured by a lively Duchess of York clone. Nobody wants to know. Canary Wharf yawns in his face. It's the end of the road for Denny, seaside exile in West Sussex. Time spools backwards into a newsreel of childhood: 'Grey pebbles. Grey gulls. Grey skies. Grey roofs. Grey seas. The most deeply unfashionable resort in Europe with a higher rainfall than Seattle.' The clapped out DHSS hotel filled with Balkan immigrants (think Hastings, think Margate), the 'barmy' old mum in the caravan, the assumed identity, the numb expectation of the only award the bureaucrats can offer for a lifetime's service: the Jack Trevor Story Memorial Prize (i.e. bankruptcy papers and an invitation to present yourself at a strip-lit office with a view of King's Cross Station). 'It's not a backwater. It's more of a septic tank.'

The necrophile damp of the South Coast, in the lull between low-pressure weather fronts, doubles for the enervating heat of the accident into which Moorcock has inserted himself: Bastrop, Texas. A good place not to go out from. A self-curated mausoleum of memories: photographs, toys, magazines, William Morris wallpaper, Arts and Crafts furniture; a library of Victorian and Edwardian fiction, Stevenson, Meredith, Wells, Conrad, W. Pett Ridge. Moorcock, with his sacred cats in a basket, brings up a map of London on his screen, shifting and rearranging co-ordinates until the city conforms to his reading of it. No longer able to potter out into Notting Hill to check on some detail, he is in the position that Robin Cook found himself in when, working in a vineyard in the South of France, he decided to reinvent himself as 'Derek Raymond'. Raymond's late London novels are pure wish fulfilment, breeze-block Piranesi: nightscapes salvaged from interrogation tapes, confessions to unremembered crimes, a dispersed set. The weather is borrowed from Edgar Wallace's quota quickies and the dialogue from Edgar Lustgarten's forensic reconstructions. A posthumous dream with a cast of greasy-tie filth and poetry-quoting psychopaths; autopsy flashbacks. Moorcock's memory scheme is more complex: bondings and rivalries, lovers and locations, have to be transported into an enriched present tense. There is a fearful momentum, snappy verbless sentences. Cast lists from afternoon television are interspersed with yarns and potted biographies, shards of ruin: get it all down or it will vanish forever. And you, the author, along with it. 'There are certain areas of London that I suspect retain their integrity and beauty only by becoming invisible.'

So the primary storyline of *King of the City*, the Candide-like fable of good-hearted Denny Dover, 'goozer' and loser, swerves away as the teller of the tale, the pretend author, is elbowed aside by the exiled Moorcock – who has to whisper in his ear, correct him, put flesh on spindly, fictional bones. The case being made is not a fashionable one: paparazzo as democratic hero, champion of the mob. 'You can't invade their privacy,' he says. 'They've sold their privacy.' Denny talks too much (and too well) for a photographer, he's altogether too articulate. But then he's also a guitarist, colleague of Bob Calvert, connection of Hawkwind, essential element in The Deep Fix: he's done things that Moorcock has done and he's picked up some of the chat.

We track Denny, son of the last Londoner hanged for murder, from his base in mythical Brookgate (part of the Huguenot leases), through a bombsite childhood reminiscent of Charles Crichton's 1947 film, *Hue and Cry* (a Moorcock favourite), through his love for his cousin Rosie and his spiky relationship with John Barbican Begg, developer and despoiler, global media tycoon. Revelations, betrayals, shifts of fortune, seductions, conspiracies, keep the fingers flicking over the pages. Dead on cue, after some cunningly weighted rhetorical passage, a jibe at 'Pretty Blair, the rich man's Cromwell,' the narrator will let rip with a great urban set-piece, like something out of Arthur Morrison, Jack London or George Gissing: a bare-knuckle boxing contest ('happy unhealthy faces glowing with meaty grease, panatella smoke'), breakfast in a Formica-table caff, a phantasmagoric binge in a Tufnell Hill windmill – which becomes an encore for the disappeared. 'You met everyone at Tubby's parties, even the recently deceased.' The party is a requiem, an expansion of Moorcock's Bastrop workspace. You can see the walls rolling back as old comrades creep out of the shadows. 'The big round living-room was festooned with cats. They lounged on every surface, across consoles and keyboards.' Time sags like the elasticated waistband on a pair of ancient Y-fronts. Arms are linked with Jack Trevor Story and Angela Carter; weird genealogies are disclosed. 'Angus Wilson, the novelist, who bore a striking resemblance to Margaret Rutherford, the actress who originally played Miss Marple,' is present. Also namechecked are Patricia Hodge, Simon Russell Beale, Giles Gordon (once Moorcock's literary agent), Andrea Dworkin and Iris Murdoch, who 'sat smiling into the middle-distance while Felix Martin explained the H-bomb to her.' What Moorcock is doing, under the permission of a work of fiction, is contriving a comprehensive encyclopaedia of lost lives, uncelebrated loci, trashed cultural memory. Every casual aside accesses a John Aubrey character sketch or a history of *Lilliput* magazine. You don't just get the word on Tommy Steele and Charlie Watts, you get Pavli and Martin Stone, once of Mighty Baby and the Savoy Brown Blues Band. 'Martin Stone hadn't been to bed for three years. His black beret was twitching on his scalp.' Behind Kingsley Amis and 'ice-cream suited' J.G. Ballard are Alan Brien, Maeve Peake, Dave Britton and legions of the erased and discontinued: Notting Hill colons, grafters, bullshitters, pharmaceutical casualties and Fleet Street drain-rats. Moorcock grants us more than any novelist is required to deliver: hence the unease of several reviewers. At times the polemic surge drowns the hesitant voices of the invented characters; they have to withdraw from the action, regroup, study their documentary models.

In *Mother London*, the author vanished into the text: the dictation, the seizure of the imagination, was absolute. There was a sense of inevitability as the past was mythologised, made new. *King of the City* is much more troubled. There is wild humour, tremendous events are staged, confessions broached, public clowns ridiculed, but you can hear the racing clockwork of a damaged heart. The crow's beak tapping on glass. Moorcock, in his Texas bunker, wants to bring what's on his desk – the cardboard city, the postcards of trams, the blown-up portions of the London map, the snapshots of a younger, beardless self – to life; he is compelled to tell it all, to remember everything. When he makes one of his brief returns to England, he is treated like a privileged ghost, a convalescent. Younger writers, attached to a sentimental notion of the heroic age of pulp, rumours of mass-market readership, have elected Moorcock as their King of the May (like Allen Ginsberg in dark ages Prague). A Prince of Thieves. It's a courtesy title: see Moorcock, in the publicity shot for the collection *britpulp!*, on his throne under the railway arches, a scarfed and hatted Fagin surrounded by smooth-cheeked, bare-headed acolytes – Tony White, Stewart Home, Steve Aylett, Steve Beard, China Miéville. What you are getting is a frame from Moorcock's comic strip, *The Metatemporal Detective*, showing a traditional 'hell's kitchen' where 'Old Man Smith,' the piratical ruler of the underworld, lounges on a raised chair to receive his tributes. Only in the labyrinth of fiction is Moorcock recognised as king of the city.

'The air has an amniotic taste.' Memory is most powerfully provoked by smell and taste. Food, more than the drink, drugs and music which act as temporal markers in the centrifugal plot, anchors narrative to place. Without those vein-clogging breakfasts, Denny Dover was lost – and his creator with him. 'They were willing me into non-existence,' he acknowledged. The older we get, the less powerful our bite, the more our reveries shift from sexual anticipation to remembered blow-outs, over-spilling plates, vinegar-brown sauces. Food and weather define the true Brookgate man, the ability to survive them, to nurture a specially adapted bio-system on draughts of bad air. 'Damp weather's food and drink to a Londoner like me,' Denny announces. 'Grey weather's our natural habitat.' In the depth of a lightless winter, a suicide's Christmas, cut off lovers and friends, 'speedballing to the Queen's Speech,' Moorcock's paparazzo recovers his humanity by drifting down to his favourite caff, Ray's, a time-warp oasis in Snatcher's Island, off Drury Lane. A bolthole discoverable only by strict adherence to the Arthur Machen rules of psychogeographic meandering.

Ray's steamy caff provokes a lascivious taxonomy of Bunter comforts, a memory sluice. The great and the good are approvingly ticked off as they stagger into Moorcock's survival module, the ark he is preparing for burial as a millennial tribute: Ronnie Scott, Humphrey Lyttelton,

Johnny Dankworth, the actor Freddie Earlle. 'Jack Trevor Story introduced me to Billy Strayhorn.' Names recalled are virtues recovered. For long stretches, *King of the City* becomes a back number of *Spotlight*, a vagrant's overcoat stitched from yellowed copies of the *Radio Times*. 'I value the approval of the forgotten dead over the respect of the living.' Denny Dover and his cousin Rosie, one of the near-incestuous bondings that have always been a part of Moorcock's novels, link souls over a plate of 'Sharpes Alley bloodworms and taters'. In Moorcock's mythical city, there are only initiates and outsiders, bloodworm-fanciers and bloodless vegans. 'To get their flavour, the worms had to be made from fresh pig's blood, which meant the pig was being hung and bled somewhere nearby, completely at odds with every city law since the beginning of the world.'

Licking the fatty residue from its beard, *King of the City* is nostalgic about nostalgia, angry about the mindless greed of developers and bingeing asset-strippers, heritage pirates; the dead rhetoric in the mouths of politicians ('Tony Blurr and his Sultans of Spin'). Moorcock champions names who are no longer there, authors he can't rescue from the swamp of oblivion. They're not in the book, in Margaret Drabble's latest edition of the *Oxford Companion to English Literature*: no Gerald Kersh, Kyril Bonfiglioli, M. John Harrison, James Sallis, Keith Roberts, Derek Raymond, Harlan Ellison. No Jack Trevor Story. Moorcock *is* there. He's included, quite generously summarised, and not just as a 'science-fiction writer of the 1960s.' But how strange it must feel, to be allowed into the club, while most of your colleagues and former collaborators, the characters around whom so much of your work has been constructed, lead an extra-curricular existence, banished from the official canon. No wonder Moorcock, one of the few novelists with a platinum disc (from his days with Hawkwind), is so uncomfortable in an age of air guitarists: the tame Blair/Clinton wild boys of the bathroom mirror. Mime masters. Party saxophonists. Purveyors of the rock and roll wannabe novel, the novel written by the rock star's best chum.

So who is the King of the City? The ambiguities of that title haunt the novel. Denny Dover is no Christopher Walken skull-cruncher, steaming his way through an Abel Ferrara revenger's tale. The global magnate, John Barbican Begg, jumps off Tower Bridge (a faked suicide) during the millennial come-back gig at the book's climax. And Moorcock, despite obvious challenges to other pretenders to the title (the literary equivalent to his bare-knuckle prizefights), is too sane to want that hollow honour. He's had his skirmishes, his turf wars with the Amis franchise. But, once again, the timing of publication has been awkward, setting *King of the City* (a secret history made of minute particulars, submerged elegies) alongside Peter Ackroyd's *London: The Biography*. Ackroyd's vigorous bestseller ends with the defeat of chaos, with protest and riot tamed. Moorcock is an unreconstructed populist, his sympathies always with the rioters at the prison gates: 'My old, sweet, darling mob. My good old London mob.' As his invented (or reinvented) revenants and anonymous extras vanish from Tower Bridge, a crush of real literary masks, PR folk, media flotsam, Dome apologists brush past them, waving their invitation cards for the launch of Ackroyd's heritage blockbuster. If they turn to gaze down at the black waters of the Thames, they won't find the drowning Begg. *King of the City* is a book they haven't read, not yet. There weren't any wine-sipping parties for Moorcock's London novel and the exiled author couldn't make it for the tour. The budget went on posters. And now the bailiffs and the fiscal bounty-hunters are on his case. 'Finances were so bad that cash machines would set off their own alarms if I so much as glanced at them. I needed somewhere to hide for a while.' Sometimes, when fly-pitchers rip off a pad of back numbers on Commercial Street, a bit of Moorcock's eye, or a clump of hair, bursts through the latest one-shot wonder's marble cheek. The message is still out there: 'Vote.' Or, better still, read, find out just what you've been missing.

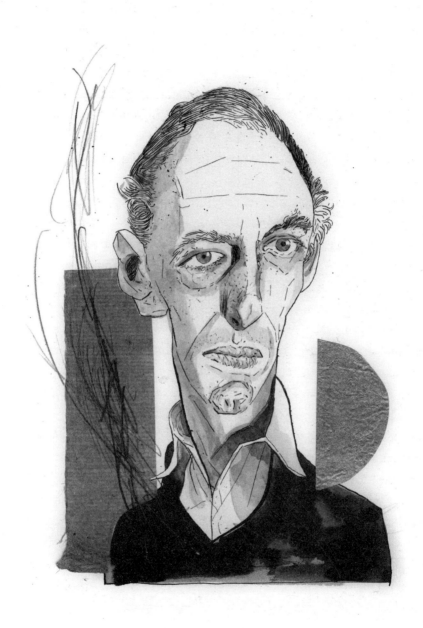

Robert Westerby

WIDE BOYS NEVER WORK (1937)

Wide Boys Never Work. We want to witness those letters in smoky light bulbs, fusing in the rain, on the side of some red Alhambra: a pastiched Hitchcock tracking shot. Robert Westerby's title has an ersatz immortality – but the author, along with all his other books and film scripts, years of Hollywood servitude (and loot), vanishes: absolutely. Charity-shop scavengers, over-the-collar hair lank with hard-travelled sweat, belted torpedo coats reeking of buses, amphetamine froth salt-white on chewed and blistered lips, would lean over my Camden Passage stall to whisper: '*Wide Boys.* Ever seen a first – in jacket? I let one go in Cecil Court, mint mint mint. O man, they stitched me up. I'll never see it again.'

Even the most memory-coshed runners have certain titles on the tips of their furred tongues – *Café-Bar, The Lowlife, Wide Boys Never Work* – while the authors are completely forgotten. This subterranean, word-of-mouth London is a bibliography of items that are always on the point of being republished, newly promoted, decades after the originals have disappeared and the poor hacks responsible, drudging for a pittance, have been banished to oblivion. Cremated in Kensal Green. Buried alive in Willesden. Misquoted in a blizzard of pseudonymous blogs on some well-intentioned website. The act of 'rescuing' lost titles is the only restitution we are prepared to make for a condition of cultural amnesia, reliance on the lazily established canon of the broadsheet reviewers and their academic sponsors.

Robert Westerby is the antithesis of all this. He types on your eyeballs with a hot needle. His language is unvarnished, stripped to essence. He has a voice you learn to trust, the tale will tell itself: damaged men in damaged times. A prose version of photo-journalism. Reportage. Significant detail. Snappy dialogue. Attitude without editorial intervention. Seedy characters frozen in the blinding flash of Weegee's ambulance-chasing camera. Murder scenes before the bad thing happens. Nothing to sell beyond its own occasion. Every published story a rejected film script.

So few people succeeded in locating a copy of *Wide Boys Never Work*, Westerby's September 1937 novel, that its status remained inviolate. The title defined a period; it enjoyed a life of its own, independent of author and the circumstances of original publication. A cultural virus, the book lodged in the private collections of later writers who made it their business to retrieve and remember. Schlepping about town as dealer in used books (libraries of the lost), I learnt that key works were scattered in musty bedrooms, heaped corridors, boxes under the stairs. Ownership was the initiation into a secret society open to all. A confederacy of gossip, rumour and misinformation: a cache of inscribed Gerald Kershs found in Morecambe by Martin Stone and sold to Michael Moorcock. Or traded for lavishly annotated Moorcock typescripts. The respected London historian, Jerry White, showed me a pristine copy of *Wide Boys* on his shelves. When I expressed my admiration, and asked him where on earth he'd found it, his reply was shocking. 'I bought it from you. Along with all those Mark Benneys.'

Ken Worpole, I'm pretty sure, had another copy. His pioneering study of working-class authors and readers, *Dockers and Detectives*, namechecks Westerby, without proffering any further information. Worpole points out that Valentine Cunningham's 'definitive' account of British writers in the 1930s makes no mention of *Wide Boys Never Work*. The novelist, filmmaker and serious collector of submerged

196

London literature, Chris Petit, acquired so many copies in variant dustwrappers that he was able to pass on his 1948 *Wide Boys* reissue (from John Lehmann's Holiday Library). Which comes with a nice little introduction by the author and a few tweaks and revisions. He now regrets his generosity in selling me Westerby's hardboiled second novel, *Only Pain is Real*, with the presentation inscription to 'Mr and Mrs Hall'. Who remain, as with so much in this story, properly mysterious.

The term 'wide boy' is a local pejorative, coming out of defensive middle-class sensibilities, to sit alongside the far uglier 'Jew boy'. Westerby's precursor of the postwar spiv, whatever the man's age, is socially immature, shirking responsibility, open to any racket. A threat to decency. A non-working working-class bum with wop tailoring and American dreams. Padded shoulders, chicken legs. Permanent fag, cutthroat razor in deep pocket. Simon Blumenfeld published *Jew Boy*, an East End right of passage, in 1935. A lot of people have read that title, very few have braved the novel. The 1930s were a great period for crime fiction, melodrama, vampiric spectres of film noir. The blackshirt in the pinball arcade. The storm-trooper in the fun house mirror. Gabardine reps, pipes primed, trade politics and smut on smoky trains.

Puffing heroically, as they return to the capital, the salesmen offer a grudging endorsement to the British fascist leader: 'Now, old Mosley. I don't like him much, but he's got the right idea about the Yids.' Westerby's protagonist, Jim Bankley, despite that subliminal 'bank' in the name, is anti-political, rather than apolitical. A disenchanted lout: 'muddy with poor food and chronic constipation... surly and anxious.' It takes Westerby a quarter of this slim novel to get his man to London. Where he will trade muscle for initiation into the tricks and subterfuges of the 'wide' world of dog tracks, clubs, car show-rooms – before returning, having 'tasted blood', to the constriction of the terraced home from which he set out.

*

Robert Westerby shares a birthday, 3 July, with Franz Kafka. That is one of the few facts the internet has to offer. Born: 1909, England. Died: 1968, California. Around a dozen books published by Arthur Barker between *Wide Boys Never Work* (1937) and *In the Money* (1952). After that it was the usual deliriously prodigal West Coast career, movie scripts for everything from *The Fighting Prince of Donegal* to King Vidor's *War and Peace*. Vehicles customised for Peter McEnery, Richard Attenborough, Audrey Hepburn. *Wide Boys* was filmed in 1956 as *Soho Incident*.

Sketchy autobiographical material can be extracted from the Westerby memoir, *A Magnum for My Mother* (1946). The title was not a reference, as Americans thought, to a handgun: no potential Don Siegel option here. The book is episodic, shaped anecdotes from a childhood spent somewhere on the fringes of London (no specifics revealed), name and rank only. A Richmal Crompton world of respectably feral kids with eccentric relatives, servants and followers, weary mother and preoccupied father (something in the City). Pointers to the author's earlier realist fictions are available to those who are prepared to dig. One of Westerby's brothers is called Jim: the first name of the protagonist of *Wide Boys*. There is a standard *Just William* episode that warps from social comedy into remembered pain. A small boy, the son of an artist, a 'queer chap' with a dead wife and 'a spectacularly violent temper,' is coerced into attempting feats of daring beyond his means. He falls from a tree and dies. He is called Eric Bankley. This unusual surname is inherited by the would-be wide boy of Westerby's most celebrated novel: the provincial labourer seduced by Jewish hustlers, motor traders from minor public schools, hardmen, whores and professional losers. By London.

'The tragedy of Eric Bankley upset us all... It was easy to assess its effect on us children, because we never discussed it... The real shocks are absorbed, and comment on them has to be excavated. We never spoke of Eric again.'

Names migrate from the actual into the fabulous, bearing their karmic burdens. Chris Petit told me that whenever he was struggling for the name of a character in one of his thrillers, he fell back on the roll-call at his prep school. Jim Bankley, surrogate brother and lost child, arrives on the pages of *Wide Boys Never Work* in a complex interweaving of autobiography and invention: a suitable vessel for inarticulate anger, furious energy and jaw-snapping boredom. Hours on a narrow bed waiting for the call to action. Awkward in his body, with 'very wide shoulders,' hair 'tightly curled, almost like a negro's,' Jim watches smoke rings climb towards the flaking yellow plaster of the ceiling. His imagination pricked and flayed by *Spicy Yarns*, a soft-porn shocker on whose lurid cover an unconscious blonde is 'sprawled backwards over the arms of a big tough mug'. Without self-love, the crab's claw, there'd be no love at all.

Wide Boys Never Work, in structure, is a traditional moral tale, an unsentimental education: the 'bad' brother quitting his home, with its narrow horizons, in search of the easy money and loose women of the capital. A quest for language and a new cast of characters: 'tarts, touts, ponces, louts, bookies, ex-pugs, petty-gangsters, perhaps a stray newspaper-reporter trying to feel tough and Metropolitan.' Westerby, as guide to the labyrinth, a detached insider with the lowdown on clubs and scams and off-limits locations, is a model for the future career of Robin Cook (Derek Raymond), another privately-miseducated malcontent of enormous charm and strategic erudition. Cook's novels of the Sixties, as lexicons of period slang, a blend of lowlife and bent establishment, were more useful than any timid researches undertaken in Wigan by patronising Cambridge Marxists under the guise of the Mass-Observation movement. Westerby prefigures Cook's performed identity as a toff in disguise (beret and clip-on Gauloise): a bar-room fixture sopping up dialogue and narrowly avoiding violence. Or incarceration. The narrative punch of *Wide Boys* echoes the as-yet-untold anecdotes of old Etonian mini-cabber and vineyard-labourer, Robin Cook. That fiver peeled from a rubber-banded roll at the dog track. The chat. 'Lo, Mory. How you doing?' Westerby achieves the rancid edge of those Derek Raymond 'Factory' novels: a posthumous nightmare, a city where it is always twilight and the dead greet the dead over curled seagull-grey sandwiches at the White City track.

Sexual encounters are arid, juiceless, necrophile. Like prizefights without the sponge and bucket. Bodies press together, half-aroused in lustful hatred, and all too conscious of damp wool, rotten armpits, sour breath, cigarette-smoke saturating tangled hair. The pubic curl in carbolic soap. The exploding geyser in the shared bathroom. Congress is urgent and instantly forgettable.

Westerby is very good on smells. Small sick men unbalanced by Freudian cigars. Attractive whores, face-powder like cheap cement, have rabbits' teeth: black lips, blue smiles. Distracted women, on handkerchief-sized dance floors, wrestle with men who don't dance: they carry too much of the street indoors. They jerk neurotically, half asleep, conscious of their blisters, to the shriek of a queer saxophonist. There is a forensic bite in Westerby's prediction of cancers flowering beneath lardy complexions. His pre-war London, balancing social and racial prejudices with authoritarian fantasy, stinks of the mob. Shaved monkeys in chalkstripe suits scratching their privates. Consumptive Welsh boxers with anthracite underwear. Sub-humans, conscientious objectors in the class war, incubate treachery and anticipate random acts of violence with masochistic relish. When razors flash and teeth are spat into sawdust, there will always be some clerk from the suburbs rutting under the table. 'Jim saw that the woman on the floor had no underclothes on. The man with her was blubbering with fear and shouting something about the police.' This is Charlotte Street imagined by George Grosz or Otto Dix. A traumatised interval between global conflicts, *Palais de Danse* dissolving into concentration camp.

The motherless Jim Bankley is a reflex misogynist, attracted to a homosexual sub-culture that also repels him. Louie Franks, his Jewish mentor, is a gay man who indulges his gauche protégée: as disposable rough trade. Jim's motor-trade boss, Graham Swing, has been expelled from his private school after 'a rather strange episode with a smaller boy in the dark room of the photographic club.' Modernist art, when it appears, is a badge of decadence: screaming queens and inane cocktail-party chatter (acid as early Eliot). 'Tony shrilled with laughter. "My *dear!*" he said. "Too *Nazi!*"' The evening ends with a failed seduction, Bankley beating the man with the nice wallpaper to an ecstatic pulp. Jim Thompson meets Francis Bacon.

Moving the narrative from a motor-manufacturing town, some-where around Birmingham, to the London of wide boys, gamblers, queers, working girls, suggests a disenchanted leftist perspective. *Wide Boys* is a product of its time, of the Spanish Civil War, thugs attacking synagogues, Oxbridge 'pylon poets' heading off to Berlin in search of the zeitgeist (and handsome blond hunks). The assembly line is both a moral value for those like old man Bankley with his thirty-eight years on the shop floor and a symbol of alienation that survives in English culture right through to Karel Reisz's 1960 film version of Sillitoe's *Saturday Night and Sunday Morning* and the cacophony of Jean-Luc Godard's visit to Cowley for *British Sounds* in 1969. But Westerby comes at his class drama from another angle, by way of American hard-boiled crime. His 1937 novel, *Only Pain Is Real*, is faux-James M. Cain, pulp Steinbeck: the road, labour riots, boxers and grifters. 'I've lived pretty hard, Van, and that's the way I'm dying.' Arthur Barker issued the book in pinkish cloth with vertical red stripes, to look exactly like the English edition of Horace McCoy's *They Shoot Horses, Don't They?*

Westerby's style is dynamic, influenced by early exposure to, and fascination with, cinema. As he reports in *A Magnum for my Mother*, 'the torrid entertainments we saw may easily have affected my growing mind... Theda Bara's death scene in *Dope... Cabinet of Dr Caligari* (which gave me nightmares for a week)... And what happened to Sylvia Breamer? And Blanche Sweet? Barbara La Marr? Or Nita Naldi?' *Wide Boys Never Work* opens to the piston-rhythms of Auden's lyrics for *Night Mail* (1936). 'Blackened chimney stacks, belching untidily like recently-fired rifles, pointed skywards.' The set-pieces at the dog track, the drinking club, the boxing ring, become standards of low-budget British cinema. You can cast the thing for yourself: Gordon Harker, Googie Withers, Jack Warner, Herbert Lom, Diana Dors, Stanley Baker. 'The youth's name is Perce, and he looks as if it would be. His face is the colour of a dirty plate, and no one has ever seen him without a half-smoked cigarette drooping from his mouth.' The young Anthony Newley with his pleading and lizardly-ancient eyes? Narcissism and melancholy.

There is a process that happens with the best writing when the author's considered and well-executed synopsis is overwhelmed by the heat of place, the savage ventriloquism of invented characters with a mythic force far beyond anything plotted in advance. It can't happen with film in the same way, you never get more than is there: the indifferent set, the inarticulate objects. In *Wide Boys Never Work*, Westerby's seething city of collisions begins to set its own agenda – and prose, which was urgent and effective within the conventions of genre fiction, takes on the vertiginous rush of L-F. Céline: the poetry of chaos. Nobody has written better about criss-crossing London, on foot and on buses, in the delirium of alcohol and electricity, exile and madness, than the shrapnel-in-the-skull race-crazed French medic. *Guignol's Band. London Bridge* (of which, scandalously, no edition has been published in England). And like Céline by whom he appears to be influenced (without perhaps having read him), Westerby abandons orthodox grammar for the flicker-cuts of single frames separated by ellipses.

'He could see the lights on the grass, the movement, the black stirring of the crowd, the excitement of everything... the car... the girl in the taxi... the faces here at the party... pale, flaccid faces, bright eyes... the smell of perfume and drink... cigarette smoke curling bluely from the ash-tray... London seemed far away... like death...'

Hallucination. Sickness. Vision. Truth.

My introductory notes for this book were unresolved but concluded, when I got the email from Robert Westerby's widow, Elizabeth. I had thought the finish might be the discovery in *A Magnum for my Mother* of a character called Sinclair, a school-fellow of Westerby's, who 'read a lot – under the sheets with an electric torch; it gave him permanently red eyes.' But Elizabeth's eye-witness report trumped all that. Robert Westerby, it seems, was working at Pinewood Studios on a Disney movie, *Three Lives of Thomasina* (1963) – Patrick McGoohan, Susan Hampshire, a 'family' picture about a cat – when Walt invited him to come to Burbank to do some rewrites. He loved California: 'the sun, beaches, playing tennis, dining, theatre and movies.' And he stayed. Lacking a green card, he chose to return once a year to England, to his 'large manor house' in Pinbury Park, Sapperton Valley, in the Cotswolds. The rural idyll. The place where John Masefield once lived.

Westerby covered a Joe Louis championship fight in Chicago in 1937 for Paramount News, but he was not a regular at the ringside and he never talked about boxing (an activity that features so much in his fiction). He relished the West Coast good life, playing table-tennis with the violin virtuoso Jascha Heifetz, socialising with Eric Ambler and King Vidor and entertaining 'people from the studios.' Thereby proving that there are second acts in English lives. Those of us who are left behind, in our imploding city, in the weather, have Westerby's early novels, crafted by a man transformed, as windows into that vanished pre-war world.

Jim Bankley, drifting aimlessly down Charing Cross Road, pauses at Foyle's window. 'What did people want so many books for, anyway? Probably only the mugs who write could tell the answer to that one.'

Iain Sinclair was born in 1943 in Cardiff, and studied at Trinity College, Dublin, the Courtauld Institute of Art, and the London School of Film Technique. His early work was poetry, published by his own Albion Village Press. He was connected to the British avant-garde poetry scene in the 1960s and 70s involving J.H. Prynne, Douglas Oliver and Brian Catling. The city of London is central to his work, and his books tell a psychogeography of London involving numerous characters such as those found in this book. His non-fiction works include *Lights Out for the Territory: 9 Excursions in the Secret History of London* (1997); *Rodinsky's Room* (1999), with Rachel Lichtenstein; *London Orbital: A Walk Around the M25* (2002); *Edge of the Orison* (2005), a reconstruction of the poet John Clare's walk from Epping Forest to Helpston, near Peterborough; and *London Overground* (2015). His novels include *Downriver* (1991); *Landor's Tower* (2001); *White Goods* (2002); *Dining on Stones* (2004); and *Hackney, That Rose-Red Empire* (2009), which was shortlisted for the 2010 Ondaatje Prize. Iain Sinclair lives in Hackney, East London.

Dave McKean is an award-winning English illustrator, graphic novelist, photographer, designer, filmmaker and musician. His work incorporates drawing, painting, photography, collage, found objects, digital art and sculpture. He has published many graphic novels, including *Black Dog: The Dreams of Paul Nash* (a 14-18 Now Foundation/Imperial War Museum/LICAF commission) and *Cages*, which was reissued in 2016 with an introduction by Terry Gilliam. He has also collaborated with Neil Gaiman, Richard Dawkins, Heston Blumenthal, Ray Bradbury, David Almond and John Cale. He has produced book and album covers for Stephen King, Roy Harper, Alice Cooper, Rolling Stones and Alan Moore, amongst many others. He has written and directed three feature films: *Mirrormask, The Gospel of Us* (two Cymru Baftas) and *Luna* (Raindance Best Feature, BIFA). Dave McKean lives on the Isle of Oxney in Kent.

Since 2006, **Tangerine Press** has published new, neglected and innovative writing in handbound limited editions, in tandem with more readily available paperbacks. The press's list includes work by William Wantling, Billy Childish, James Kelman, Jack London, Iain Sinclair, Akiko Yosano, Stephen Hines, Hone Tuwhare, &c.